Sew Sweet Creatures

Make adorable plush animals
and their accessories

LARK

New York

⟨≋LARK
New York

LARK CRAFTS and the distinctive Lark logo
are registered trademarks of Sterling Publishing Co., Inc.

© 2015 by Sterling Publishing
Illustrations by Orrin Lundgren
Photography by Christopher Bain

ISBN 978-1-4547-0890-2

Distributed in Canada by Sterling Publishing
c/o Canadian Manda Group, 664 Annette Street
Toronto, Ontario, Canada M6S 2C8
Distributed in the United Kingdom by GMC Distribution Services
Castle Place, 166 High Street, Lewes, East Sussex, England BN7 1XU
Distributed in Australia by Capricorn Link (Australia) Pty. Ltd.
P.O. Box 704, Windsor, NSW 2756, Australia

For information about custom editions, special sales, and premium
and corporate purchases, please contact Sterling Special Sales at
800-805-5489 or specialsales@sterlingpublishing.com.

Manufactured in China

2 4 6 8 10 9 7 5 3 1

larkcrafts.com

CONTENTS

INTRODUCTION

The sixteen plush creatures presented in these pages are undeniably cute, and the talented designers who have contributed these projects have taken handmade plush animals to the next level of adorableness, as each project includes a number of creative accessories. How can you resist the sweet Adventurer Bear who is ready for a trip with a camera, backpack, and map; Anna the Snuggly Llama, with socks, a fleece blanket, and hat; or the charming Superhero Pig with a cape and mask?

The best gifts are personal and heartfelt, and the projects in *Sew Sweet Creatures* can't help but warm the heart. Make these plush critters as a gift for a new mom, a decorative keepsake to treasure, or a cuddly toy for your own child. Each critter has a story and carries accessories to go with it. Read the stories to your children, have them choose their favorite creature, and then make them each their very own personalized plush animal.

Feel free to add your own personal touches, or switch accessories between projects—the Adventurer Bear could become a Festival Bear, or the Superhero Pig a Fairy Pig. The variations and entertainment are endless.

Have fun and enjoy making your own sweet plush creatures to love!

NOTE
If you are planning to give a project to a young child, please stitch eyes and other details on to the stuffed animal instead of using buttons, beads, or any other small decorative items that may pose a choking hazard. See page xi for tips on using stitches to create details.

BASICS
Basic Materials and Tools

Each project will require a variety of specific materials and tools, but there are a few core items that are essential to any basic sewing kit. Be sure to have these standard tools on hand, and check each project's Materials and Tools lists to make sure you have everything you need before you begin.

EMBROIDERY FLOSS

FABRIC GLUE

GLUE STICK

STUFFING

THREAD

NEEDLES
(EMBROIDERY AND HAND-SEWING)

ERASABLE FABRIC MARKER
OR FABRIC PENCILS

SCISSORS (CRAFT AND FABRIC)

STRAIGHT PINS

TURNING TOOL

PINKING SHEARS

RULER / MEASURING TAPE

SEAM RIPPER

SEWING MACHINE

IRON

Backstitch

To create a backstitch, make a straight stitch from A to B, then bring your needle back through the fabric a short distance away at point C ahead of the first stitch and ending at stitch A. See illustration below.

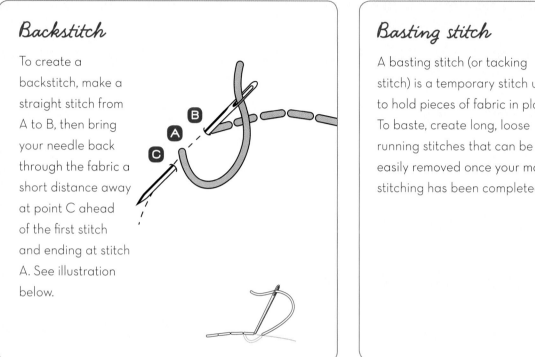

Basting stitch

A basting stitch (or tacking stitch) is a temporary stitch used to hold pieces of fabric in place. To baste, create long, loose running stitches that can be easily removed once your main stitching has been completed.

Blanket Stitch

Blanket stitch, also known as buttonhole stitch, makes a pretty, decorative stitch for borders or edges. Make a diagonal stitch from point A to B. Bring the needle up again at point C, catching the lower loop of the thread under the needle as you make the parallel straight stitches.

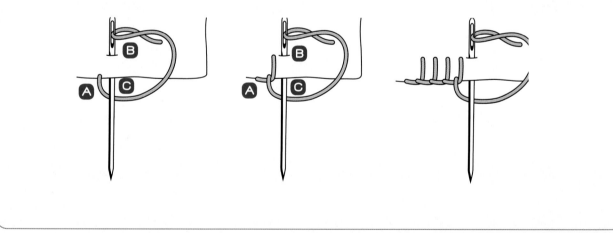

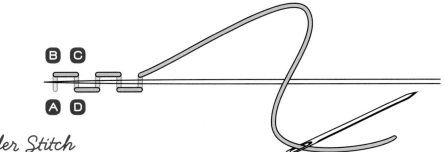

Ladder Stitch

Ladder stitch, also known as blind or hidden stitch, is a nearly invisible stitch perfect for sewing seams in pillows or plush projects that already have been stuffed. To ladder stitch, bring the needle and thread through the back of the fabric at point A and then back down across the opening at point B. Slide the needle along the opening in the fabric and pull it out at point C. Reinsert the needle across from point C at point D and pull the thread tightly. Continue along the opening to close the seam.

Running Stitch

Also known as straight stitch or seed stitch, running stitch is very simple. Push your needle and thread in through the back of the fabric at point A, push back down at point B, and repeat. You can also add running stitches in groupings to create small details like eyes, mouths, or fur.

Stab Stitch

With this stitch, the needle is "stabbed" into the front of the fabric, then pulled through the fabric from the other side.

Topstitch

A topstitch is sewn parallel to a seam or along a hem on the right side of the fabric. It is the most common of sewing machine stitches.

Whipstitch

To whipstitch, simply stitch over and around the edge of the two pieces of fabric to create a seam. Hold the two pieces of fabric together as you stitch the edge.

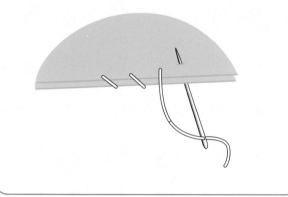

Woven Backstitch

Start at one end of the line of backstitches (see viii) and weave the needle and thread back and forth through the line on the front of the fabric. Go up through one backstitch and down through the next.

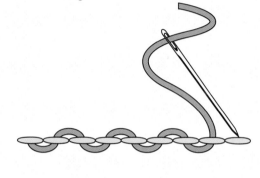

Zigzag Stitch

This is a common back-and-forth sewing machine stitch but can also be done by hand. It's a great finishing stitch for the edges of seam allowances.

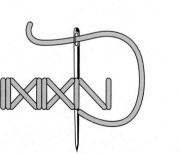

Satin Stitch

Use satin stitch to create a solid, smooth, raised area of fill stitches to create a shiny nose. To satin stitch, bring your needle and thread up through the back of the fabric and make a straight stitch, then make a second straight stitch directly next to it, a little longer or shorter as needed. Continue this process until you have filled the intended space with parallel stitches to create a smooth, shiny, raised surface.

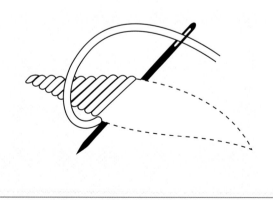

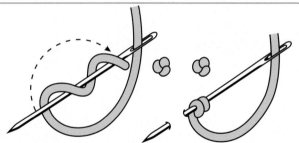

French Knot

Knot stitches like the French Knot, are great for creating eyes. To create a French Knot, bring your needle up through the back of the fabric where you would like the knot to appear. Pull the thread through until the knot is against the back of the fabric. Wrap the thread tightly over and around the needle three or four times, keeping the needle near the surface of the fabric. (To create a smaller knot, wrap the thread around the needle just two times.) Slide the loops down closer to the tip of the needle, then push the needle back down into the cloth close to the place where the needle came up. Be sure to pinch the loops in place as you push the needle through the fabric. Pull the needle completely through the cloth and the French Knot will form at the front.

Clipping Curves

Clipping fabric at curved seams allows for smooth and even curves and corners of pieces that will be turned right side out. After you have sewn a seam, simply cut a series of small triangular notches along the seam allowance before turning the piece right side out.

Stretch Markings

A few of the projects in this book reference "stretch markings." Fabric usually has more stretch in one direction than the other. The stretch marking arrows are noted on specific project templates and depict the direction in which the fabric should be positioned to account for the fabric's stretch. Be sure to position the pieces of fabric according to the direction of the greatest stretch before cutting the pieces using the templates.

Using Embroidery Floss to Create Details

A variety of embroidery stitches may be used to create small details on your creatures to avoid using buttons or other small decorative items, which may pose a choking hazard for small children.

Running Stitch

You can use running stitches to create a dashed line—perfect for critter mouths or any other linear details. You can also use running stitches to make groupings of dashes to create texture for a fur-like appearance. See the running stitch illustration on page (ix).

Appliqué

Appliqué is a technique in which a layer—or layers—of fabric are attached, or applied to the surface of another, larger piece of fabric. Common stitches used to appliqué are the blanket stitch, running stitch and whipstitch.

> ### NOTE
> Most projects in this book will specify which particular stitches should be used for specific steps. If a stitch is not specified, feel free to hand-sew or use your machine—whichever method you prefer!

The PROJECTS

ADVENTURER BEAR

DESIGNER: JESSICA FEDIW

This bear is the perfect adventure buddy. He loves to explore and take pictures during his travels. He is small enough to fit in your pocket and is ready to start exploring with a map that rolls up to be put in his backpack and a camera to take pictures of things he sees and likes. He loves to go on adventures, make new friends along the way, and discover new things.

MATERIALS

Templates (page 66–67)

Cotton fabric for the bear's body, ¼ yard (22.9 cm)

Felt in light brown for the bear's tummy, nose, and paw prints; in blue for the backpack and straps; and small scraps of brown, blue, green, and light brown felt for the map, one sheet of each color

Coordinating sewing thread

Embroidery floss in blue, black, and white

Stuffing

Fabric glue

Craft glue

Black dimensional fabric paint

Yarn, 6 inches (15.2 cm)

Piece of wood, 1 x 1 ¼ inches (2.5 x 3.2 cm)

Wooden spool, ³/₄ x 1 inch (1.9 x 2.5 cm)

Black and white craft paint

Leather cord, 7 inches (17.8 cm), ⅛-inch wide (3 mm)

Small button for the backpack, ½-inch (1.3 cm) in diameter

TOOLS

Fabric scissors

Hand-sewing needle

Embroidery needle

Sewing machine

Turning tool, ³/₈ inch (9.5 mm) in diameter

Straight pins

Iron

NOTE:
All seam allowances are ¼ inch (6 mm) unless otherwise specified.

INSTRUCTIONS

Make the Bear

1 Use the templates to cut two body pieces, four ears, and eight hands/feet from the fabric. Cut one tummy, one nose, and two sets of paw prints from the light brown felt.

2 Center the felt tummy on the front of the body. Sew in place. Center the felt nose on the middle of the face and sew in place using matching thread.

3 Embroider the eyes, nose, and mouth on the face.

4 Pin two ear pieces together, right sides facing. Sew them together, leaving the straight end open. Cut notches in the seam allowances on the curves (see page xi). Turn right side out and press.

5 Sew the paw prints onto the front of two hand pieces; they should be placed in far enough to avoid being sewn into the seam allowance. Pin one paw-print hand to a blank one, right sides facing. Sew together, leaving the straight end open. Cut notches in the seam allowance around the curves. Repeat for the other paw and for the two feet. Turn each one right side out and stuff, leaving ½ inch (1.3 cm) empty at the open end.

6 Pin the ears, hands, and feet onto the front body piece, right sides facing. Sew them in place as close to the edge as possible.

7 Pin the back body piece onto the front piece, right sides facing. Sew them together, leaving an opening between the two feet for turning. Cut notches in the seam allowance at the curves. Turn right side out and stuff. Turn in the opening edges and then hand-sew it closed with whipstitch.

Make the Map

Use the map template to cut out the map rectangle from brown felt. Cut out other small shapes for trees, lakes, and mountains from the other colors of felt. Glue the small shapes onto the map. Use dimensional paint to make small lines that indicate a trail; let dry. Fold yarn in half and glue the fold to the opposite side of the map on one end. Cut a small piece of felt to glue on top of the yarn's fold to cover it. When the glue is dry, the map can be rolled up and tied with the yarn.

Make the Camera

Paint the wooden piece and the spool black. Once dry, glue the spool onto the center of the wood piece. Paint a small dab of white where a camera flash would be. Let dry. Glue each end of the leather cord to the back of the camera on opposite sides.

Make the Backpack

Cut out the backpack and strap pieces from the blue felt using the templates provided. Sew the straps onto the top and bottom sides of the middle portion. Fold the straight end of the backpack up where indicated on the template. Sew the sides down. Hand-sew a button of your choice onto the front of the backpack. Fold down the top to determine where to cut a hole for the button; cut a slit big enough for the button to go through.

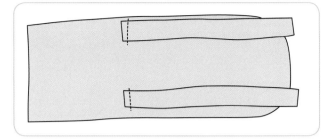

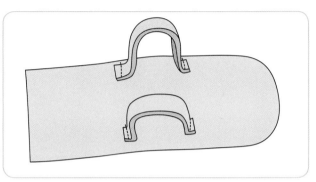

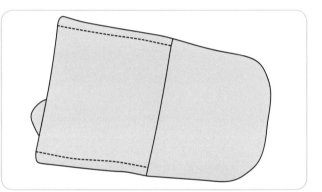

EMBROIDERY TIPS

To make the bear's eyes, begin by sewing an x, then sew a line connecting each end of the x to another. For the nose, first embroider the outer edges and then fill it in.

ANNA THE SNUGGLY LLAMA

DESIGNER: MOLLIE JOHANSON

Poor Anna! She might be a llama with a furry coat, but she's still always cold! To help her warm up and stay snuggly, her family got her some fancy socks, a woolly hat, and a beautiful blanket from Peru, where her ancestors came from. Now Anna is feeling a lot warmer! Don't worry though—even if she doesn't have her hat, blanket, or socks, Anna always has a warm heart and would be happy to snuggle with you!

MATERIALS

Templates (page 68-70)
Cream fleece, ⅓ yard (30.5 cm)
Brown flannel, ¼ yard (22.9 cm)
2 pieces of lavender felt, 6 x 12 inches (15.2 x 30.5 cm) for the hat, and 9 x 9 inches (22.9 x 22.9 cm) for the socks
Light green felt, 4 x 8 inches (10.2 x 20.3 cm)
Sewing thread in coordinating colors
Brown, purple, and green embroidery floss
Two 9 mm safety eyes
Stuffing
Tracing paper

TOOLS

Scissors
Erasable fabric pen
Embroidery needle
Straight pins
Sewing machine
Hand-sewing needle

INSTRUCTIONS
Make the Llama

1 Using the templates, cut two body pieces from the fleece and transfer the markings for the face onto one piece. Be sure to follow the stretch marking (see page xi). Cut eight leg pieces from the flannel. Cut four ear/tail pieces from the fleece and two ear/tail pieces from the flannel. Cut one muzzle piece from the flannel, adding a ¼-inch (6 mm) seam allowance.

2 On the front body piece, cut two tiny holes where the eyes will go and install the safety eyes. (If you will be giving this to a young child, embroider or appliqué the eyes instead.)

3 Embroider the nose and mouth on the muzzle. Make a basting stitch (page ix) around the muzzle with embroidery floss, then, holding the muzzle template (without the added seam allowance) on the back of

NOTE: All seam allowances are ¼ inch (6 mm).

the embroidered muzzle, pull the running stitch to gather it around the template, and secure the thread with a knot. Finger-press the edges and remove the paper template. Stitch the muzzle to the front body piece with running stitch.

④ Pin two leg pieces with right sides together and sew around the sides and bottom, leaving the straight edge open for turning. Repeat with all sets of legs. Do the same with the ear and tail pieces. Turn all of the pieces right side out. Add stuffing to the leg pieces.

⑤ Place the back body piece right side up, then lay the ears, tail, and legs on top, raw edges aligning with the edge of the body piece and the finished sides facing in. Baste the pieces in place.

⑥ Pin the front body piece to the back with right sides together. Sew around the sides, leaving an opening for turning. Clip the curves (see page xi), then turn the body right side out. Stuff the body, and sew the opening closed with ladder stitch (page ix).

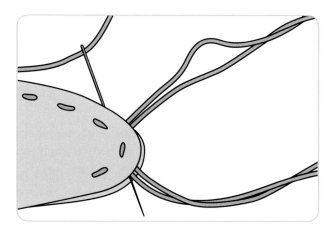

Make the Hat

① Cut two hat pieces from lavender felt.

② Embroider the design (see template) on one of the pieces using backstitch (page viii) and woven backstitch (page x). To stitch it onto the felt, trace the design onto tracing paper, pin the paper on the felt, then stitch through the felt and paper; when finished, carefully tear away the paper.

③ Stitch the two hat pieces together along the sides with running stitch, leaving the openings for Anna's ears to fit through.

④ For each tie, cut two 12-inch (30.5 cm) pieces of purple embroidery floss, fold each one in half, and loop them over one of the running stitches. Braid the doubled threads and tie a knot at the end. Repeat for the other side.

Make the Blanket

Cut the blanket piece on the fold from light green felt. Embroider the design (see template) onto one or both side(s) of the blanket using the method above. Use backstitch, woven backstitch, and running stitch.

Make the Socks

Cut eight sock pieces from lavender felt. Embroider the design (see template) onto four of the sock pieces using the method above. Stitch each plain sock piece to an embroidered sock piece using running stitch.

CHIP THE LUMBERJACK BEAVER

DESIGNER: MOLLIE JOHANSON

All of the beavers in Chip's family chew down trees and build homes with the logs, but Chip likes to do so in style! That's why he wears his plaid hat and carries an axe. At first all of the other beavers thought it was a little odd, but they now know that when it comes to lumberjack beavers, Chip is okay!

MATERIALS

Templates (page 71–73)
Medium brown flannel, ¼ yard (22.9 cm)
Dark brown fleece, 8 x 11 inches (20.3 x 27.9 cm)
Plaid flannel, 8 x 14 inches (20.3 x 35.6 cm)
Cream fleece, 3 x 8 inches (7.6 x 20.3 cm)
Medium brown flannel, 6 ½ x 9 inches
    (16.5 x 22.9 cm; can be cut from
    ¼ yard [22.9 cm] above)
Tan felt, 3 x 6 inches (7.6 x 15.2 cm)
Red felt, 2 x 4 inches (5.1 x 10.2 cm)
Gray felt, 2 x 3 inches (5.1 x 7.6 cm)
Felt scraps in black and white
Thread
Embroidery floss in black, white, and red
Two 9 mm safety eyes
Stuffing
Cotton swab
Fabric glue
2 small strips of hook-and-loop fastener

TOOLS

Scissors
Erasable fabric pen
Embroidery needle
Hand-sewing needle
Straight pins
Sewing machine
Turning tool

> **NOTE**
> All seam allowances are ¼ inch (6 mm).

INSTRUCTIONS

Make the Beaver

1 Cut two body pieces from the medium brown flannel and transfer the markings for the face onto one piece. Cut two in-seam arm pieces, two front arm pieces, and four foot pieces from medium brown flannel. Cut two tail pieces from the dark brown fleece.

2 On the front body piece, cut two small holes where the eyes will go and install the safety eyes. (If you will be giving this to a young child, embroider or appliqué the eyes instead.) Cut the nose piece from the black felt and the mouth piece from the white felt using the templates provided. Appliqué the nose and teeth in place using whipstitch (page x) and matching embroidery floss, and embroider the mouth using backstitch (page viii) and black embroidery floss.

3 Pin the two in-seam arm pieces with right sides together and sew around the sides, leaving the straight edge open for turning. Repeat with the foot and tail pieces. For the front arm piece, pin and sew the pieces right sides together and leave a small opening along one of the longer sides for turning. Turn all of the pieces right side out and stuff. Stitch the front arm closed with ladder stitch (page ix).

4 Place the back body piece right side up, then lay the in-seam arm, feet, and tail on top, with raw edges aligning with the edge of the body piece and the finished sides facing in. Baste the pieces in place.

5 Fold the tail in, then pin the front body piece to the back with right sides together. Sew around the sides, leaving an opening for turning. Clip the curves (see page xi), then turn the body right side out. Stuff the body and sew the opening closed with ladder stitch.

6 Center the front arm on the body and hand-sew it in place with an oval of ladder stitch. Go around the oval two times for more security. Tie off the thread, hiding the knot between the arm and the body.

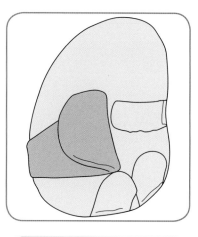

Make the Hat

1 Cut two hat pieces, two earflap pieces, and one front flap piece from the plaid flannel. Cut two earflap pieces and one front flap piece from the cream fleece. Pin the hat pieces with right sides together and sew around the curved edge. Pin a flannel earflap piece to a fleece earflap piece, right sides together, and sew around the curved edge. Repeat with the other earflap and front flap pieces. Turn all of the pieces right side out.

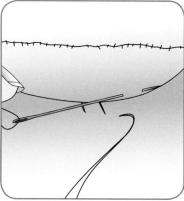

2 On the hat piece, fold a ³⁄₈-inch (9.5 mm) hem to the wrong side. Pin the three flap pieces to the inside of the hat with the flat edges up and the flannel sides facing out. Place the front flap ½ inch (1.3 cm) in from the left edge, one earflap ½ inch (1.3 cm) in from the right edge front, and the other earflap ½ inch (1.3 cm) in from the right edge on the back side of the hat. Stitch along the hem with a running stitch (page ix) to hold the hem and attach the flaps. Fold the front flap up and tack in place with a few hidden stitches.

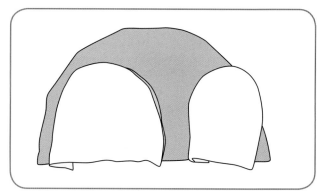

Make the Axe

Cut three handle pieces from red felt and two head pieces from gray felt. Stitch the bottom edge of two handle pieces together. Stitch the top edge of one of the pieces to the second piece about ³⁄₄ inch (1.9 cm) from the top; this will form a loop for Chip's arm to slide through. Using running stitch, attach the third handle piece to the unlooped side of the handle, leaving the top open. Push the cotton swab into the handle. Sandwich the axe head pieces around the top

of the handle and stitch around the head, catching the handle with several stitches.

Make the Log

Cut two 9 x 3 ¼-inch (22.9 x 8.3 cm) rectangles from flannel and four log end pieces from tan felt. Pin the short ends of a rectangle with right sides together.

Sew in 1 inch (2.5 cm) on each side, leaving a gap in the middle. Pin a log end into the tube and hand-sew with tiny running stitches. Repeat with the other end, making sure to turn and stuff the log before sewing closed. Make a second log piece, then glue hook-and-loop fastener to the log pieces so they can stick together and then be "chopped."

CRAFTY BUNNY

DESIGNER: LAURA HOWARD

Alex the Crafty Bunny loves to knit and sew! She's never happier than when she's making things, and she can't resist buying pretty fabric, yarn, and buttons to add to her craft stash. Her stylish knitting bag means she can take her current projects with her wherever she travels—you can often spot her knitting on the train on the way to work or in cafés on her days off. She's recently taken up dressmaking and is modeling one of her creations here. She believes in "waste not, want not" so she used bits of fabric leftover from making her dress to make a patchwork quilt. The quilt is perfect for cozy evenings while doing a bit of knitting or reading a crafty magazine or a book by one of her favorite craft bloggers.

MATERIALS

Templates (page 74–75)

Light brown felt, two 9 x 12-inch
    (22.9 x 30.5 cm) sheets

Pale pink felt, approximately 3 x 3 ½ inches
    (7.6 x 8.9 cm)

Small pieces of white, black, and aqua blue
    (or to match the dress fabric) felt

Blue floral print cotton fabric for the dress,
    approximately 12 x 24 inches (30.5 x 61 cm)
    or one fat quarter

7 additional fabrics (pink and blue floral prints or
    other prints and colors chosen to coordinate with
    the dress fabric) for the quilt, each approximately
    4 x 8 inches (10.2 x 20.3 cm)

Thick white felt (2–3 mm thick), approximately 9 x 9
    inches (22.9 x 22.9 cm)

Candy pink felt, approximately 4½ x 5½ inches
    (11.4 x 14 cm)

Light brown, pale pink, white, black, and aqua blue
    (or to match the dress fabric) sewing thread

Black, white, and 4 or 5 additional skeins in a variety
    of colors of stranded embroidery floss

3 aqua blue mini buttons, ⅜ of an inch (1 cm)
    in diameter (or to match the main dress fabric)

2 pink mini buttons

Stuffing

White yarn

Brightly colored plastic measuring tape or ribbon,
    approximately ½ inch (1.3 cm) wide and
    7½ inches (19 cm) long

2 glass beads (large enough to fit on the ends of the
    cocktail sticks)

Glue sticks or strong craft glue

2 wooden toothpicks

TOOLS

Scissors

Soft marking pencil

Small, sharp embroidery scissors

Hand-sewing needle

Embroidery needle

Straight pins

Iron

Pinking shears

Turning tool or pencil

Large, sharp sewing needle

Scrap cardboard (e.g., from a cereal box) and clear
    tape or a small pompom-making tool

Paper or craft scissors

Hot glue gun (optional)

INSTRUCTIONS

Make the Bunny

1 Use the templates to cut out the head, arms, legs, eyes, nose, teeth, ears, inner ears, collar, and pocket from the felt. Also cut two small circles from black felt for the pupils. Trace around the dress template with a soft pencil, marking the shape on the back of a piece of floral fabric, and cut it out, leaving ½-inch (1.3 cm) seam allowance around the dress shape. Turn the dress template over and repeat to cut out the second dress shape.

> ## TIP
> **To cut small felt circles for the pupils, cut a small square of felt in a spiral motion, turning the felt while cutting to create a circle. Small, sharp embroidery scissors are perfect for cutting out small shapes like this.**

2 Sew the eyes, pupils, nose, and teeth, one by one, onto one of the bunny heads with whipstitch (page x) and matching sewing threads. After sewing on the teeth, use backstitch (page viii) and white sewing thread to stitch a vertical line down the middle of the shape, dividing it into two teeth.

3 Cut a length of black embroidery floss and separate half the strands (i.e., for six-stranded floss, use three strands). Use this floss to backstitch the bunny's mouth, as pictured. Then cut a length of white embroidery floss, separate half the strands, and use them

to sew six single stitches for the whiskers.

4 Pin the pale-pink inner ear pieces to two light brown ear pieces as pictured. Sew them in place using whipstitch and matching pale-pink sewing thread, then remove the pins. Leave the bottom edges unstitched.

5 Place the front and back ear pieces together and join the edges with whipstitch and matching light brown sewing thread. Leave the bottom edges unstitched and set the ears aside until later.

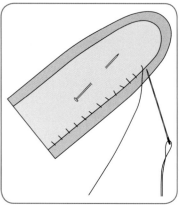

6 Fold the top ½-inch (1.3 cm) seams of the dress pieces over, pressing them flat with an iron. Pin the front and back dress pieces to the front and back bunny head shapes, respectively. Sew along the top edges of the fabric with whipstitch and aqua blue sewing thread (or one matching the dress fabric), then remove the pins.

7 Arrange the arm and leg pieces as pictured, sandwiching them between the two dress pieces (with the right sides of the fabric facing each other). Pin the layers together so the felt shapes are secured in what will be the seam of the dress.

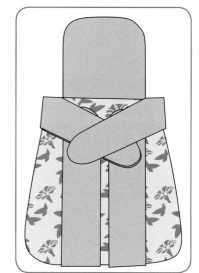

8 Follow the line marked on the fabric in pencil to sew the dress pieces together. Use matching sewing thread and small running stitches (page ix), sewing the arms and legs securely into the seam.

9 Use pinking shears to trim the excess felt and fabric from around the dress seam, taking care not to cut too close to the stitching.

10 Turn the dress the right side out, carefully pulling the fabric and felt through the neck hole at the top of the dress. Then use a pencil or other turning tool to gently poke out the bottom corners of the dress to their correct shape.

11 Add the aqua blue collar and pocket to the front of the dress. Use matching aqua sewing thread and a running stitch, taking care to sew only through the front layer of the dress. Leave the top edge of the pocket unstitched.

12 Sew a row of three aqua blue mini buttons to the back of the dress, using a double thickness of matching aqua sewing thread. Again, take care to sew only through one layer of the dress.

> **TIP**
> For an extra-neat finish, take care to sew the buttons so the holes line up with each other.

13 Using whipstitch and matching light brown thread, sew and stuff the arms and legs, one by one. Start where the limb meets the dress fabric, stitch down toward the curved end, then stuff the shape gradually while sewing back up the second side. Add small pieces of stuffing at a time, filling the legs and arms firmly.

14 Make a white pompom (see instructions below) for the bunny's tail, leaving two yarn ends sticking out from the pompom. Thread a large, sharp needle with one of these strands of yarn then sew it through the back of the bunny's dress. Repeat this with the second strand, as pictured. Knot the yarn ends together securely (without pulling so tightly that you pucker the dress fabric), then carefully trim the excess yarn.

15 Stuff the dress firmly, adding small pieces of stuffing at a time.

16 Pin the bunny's head together, with the ears inserted at the top. Begin sewing around the head with whipstitch and matching light brown sewing thread, removing the pins when they are no longer needed. Leave a gap for stuffing.

17 Stuff the bunny's head firmly, adding small pieces of stuffing at a time. Sew up the remaining gap with more whipstitches and matching thread.

Make the Pompom

Use a store-bought pompom-making tool to make a pompom measuring about 1 ½ inches (3.8 cm) in diameter, or follow these steps:

1 Trace around the ring template provided, drawing two rings onto scrap cardboard (cardboard from a cereal box is ideal for this; it should be sturdy but still flexible). Carefully cut out each ring, then use clear adhesive tape to stick the cardboard together where the center circles were cut.

2 Cut long pieces of yarn and wrap them around the rings until they are evenly covered. Use a double or triple thickness of yarn to speed the process. The more yarn you add, the fuller the pompom will be. Then cut an extra piece of yarn and set it aside.

3 Hold the ring tightly and use a pair of sharp scissors to cut around the edge of the ring, snipping through all the yarn. Keep a firm hold on the center of the ring.

4 Take the piece of yarn cut earlier in step 2 (still holding the ring firmly) and wrap it between the two layers of cardboard and around the yarn, tying it tightly and knotting it securely.

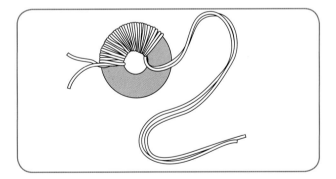

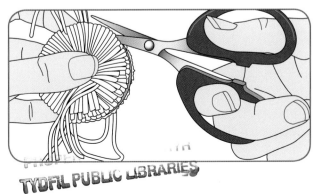

5 Remove the cardboard rings carefully. Neaten the pompom with scissors, trimming any uneven areas and leaving the two long strands of yarn in place.

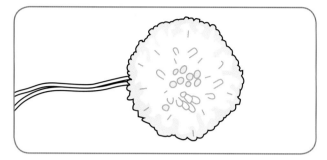

Make the Quilt

1 Use the large quilt square template to cut 16 squares from coordinating floral fabric, including two squares cut from the same fabric used for the dress. Then use the smaller square template and a soft pencil to draw the square shape centered on the back of each piece. These smaller squares will be the stitching lines to sew the quilt together. Arrange the squares in the order wanted for the quilt.

2 Pin two squares together with the right sides facing. Stitch along the pencil line with white sewing thread and small running stitches, then remove the pin. Sew more squares together in the same way, creating a row of four squares. Repeat to create four rows.

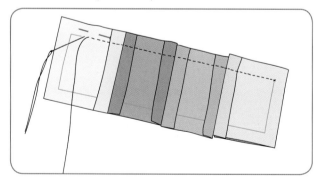

3 Use a hot iron to press the seams flat. Pin two rows together, right sides facing. Sew along the marked line with more white thread and running stitch. Remove the pins and press the seams flat. Repeat to add the other two rows.

4 Press all the seams flat. Fold and press the outer edges inward, pinning them in place. Use contrasting sewing thread and large tacking stitches to secure the fabric, folding the corners in neatly and avoiding sewing too close to the edges. Then remove the pins.

5 Cut an 8-inch (20.3 cm) square from thick white felt and a 10-inch (25.4 cm) square of the floral-print fabric. Fold the edges of the fabric over the edges of the felt, pinning and then tacking them in place. Remove the pins.

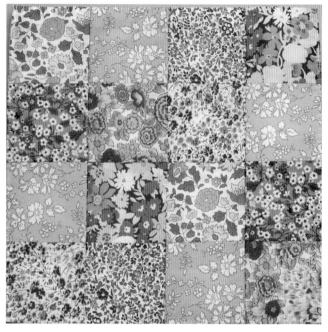

> **TIP**
> The back of the quilt needs to be the same size as the front, so measure the patchwork to check that it is 8 inches (20.3 cm) square. If it's a different size, use those measurements to cut the felt.

6 Pin the front and back of the quilt together. Use white sewing thread and blanket stitch (page viii) to sew the edges together, removing the pins as you come to them, as they are no longer needed. Then remove the tacking stitches.

Make the Knitting Bag

1 Use the bag templates provided to cut out the three pieces of candy pink felt, as marked.

2 Join one of the bag sides to the bag base using small whipstitches and matching pink sewing thread. Repeat to sew the second side to the base, then trim any excess felt.

3 Whipstitch the sides together. Turn the bag the right side out.

4 Cut a piece of plastic measuring tape about 6½ inches (16.5cm) long. Sew the ends of the tape to the sides of the bag using a double thickness of pink thread and a couple of small stitches.

TIP
If using ribbon instead of measuring tape, cut this slightly longer, about 7 ½ inches (19 cm). Fold over ½ inch (1.3 cm) at each end, securing the folded ends with a couple of small stitches of matching sewing thread.

5 Use a double thickness of pink thread to add a pink mini button to both sides of the bag.

Make the Knitting Needles

Each knitting needle is made from a wooden toothpick with a glass bead glued on the end. Choose glass beads that just fit on the toothpick.

Use a hot glue gun to apply a small drop of glue to the hole of one of the beads, then quickly push the toothpick into the hole. Repeat to make the second knitting needle. Let the glue set completely.

TIP
Attaching the beads to the toothpicks can be a little tricky, as the hot glue hardens quickly. Practice on some spare beads and toothpicks before using your final materials. You can use a strong craft glue in place of the glue gun and glue sticks.

Make the Yarn Balls

For each one, simply wind a skein of embroidery floss into a small ball.

FAIRY MOUSE

DESIGNER: LAURA HOWARD

Olivia the Fairy Mouse is here to grant your wishes! She works the night shift as a tooth fairy a few nights a week, but what she loves most of all is using her wand to grant special wishes to those in need. Her happy-go-lucky personality is just as sparkly as her wings, and nothing makes her happier than helping out the other animals whenever she can. Her favorite time of year is Christmas, when she catches up with all the Christmas fairies and helps them spread festive sparkle and cheer. When she's not collecting teeth or granting wishes, Olivia puts her wings and wand away in a safe place for the evening and goes dancing. Her pretty dress is just the thing for attending all the fanciest parties!

MATERIALS

Templates (page 76–78)
Gray felt, two 9 x 12-inch (22.9 x 30.5 cm) sheets
Lilac felt, one 9 x 12-inch (22.9 x 30.5 cm) sheet
Pale lilac felt, one 9 x 12-inch (22.9 x 30.5 cm) sheet
Pale pink felt, approximately 4 x 5 inches (10.2 x 12.7 cm)
Small pieces of white, black, and candy pink felt
Gray, lilac, pale lilac, pale pink, white, black, and candy pink sewing thread
Pale pink and white stranded embroidery floss
Stuffing
Small silver snap fastener, $3/16$ inch (5 mm) in diameter or smaller
Silver rickrack, approximately 20 inches (50.8 cm)
Silver sequins, approximately $1/4$ inch (6 mm) in diameter, approximately 220 sequins
White card stock
Glue stick
Lilac yarn
Pipe cleaner

TOOLS

Fabric scissors
Paper or craft scissors
Ruler
Straight pins
Hand-sewing needle
Sharp, small embroidery scissors
Erasable fabric marker
Pencil or other narrow stuffing tool
Large, sharp needle

INSTRUCTIONS

Make the Mouse

1 Use the templates provided to cut out the body, eye, nose, ear, tail, and top pieces from felt. Also cut out three rectangles from lilac felt, two measuring 3 x 8½ inches (7.6 x 21.6 cm) for the skirt and one measuring ⁹⁄₁₆ x 9 inches (1.4 x 22.9 cm) for the belt.

2 Turn over one body shape; this will become the back of the mouse. Place the front and back top pieces on the front and back body shapes, respectively, and then pin them in position. Whipstitch (page x) the tops in place with matching lilac sewing thread, leaving the outside edges unstitched and removing the pins when they are no longer needed.

3 Turn over one of the ear pieces; this will be stitched to the mouse's right ear. Cut two small circles from black felt for the pupils. One by one, position the eyes, pupils, ears, and nose on the front of the mouse and whipstitch them in place with matching sewing threads.

> ### TIP
> **To make small felt circles, cut a small square of felt then in a spiral motion, turning the felt while cutting to create a circle. Small, sharp embroidery scissors are perfect for cutting out small shapes like this.**

4 Cut a length of pale pink embroidery floss and a length of white embroidery floss. Separate half the strands (i.e., for six-stranded floss, use three strands). Use an air-erasable fabric marker to draw the mouse's mouth and six whiskers, as pictured. Then follow the lines with backstitch (page viii), using pink floss for the mouth and white floss for the whiskers.

5 Pin the two tail pieces together and begin sewing around the edges using small whipstitches and matching pale pink sewing thread, starting at the top corner and working down toward the tip of the tail.

6 Sew back up the other side of the tail, stuffing it gradually. Use a pencil or turning tool to help poke the stuffing into the small shape. When the tail is fully stuffed, finish sewing up the remaining gap with more whipstitches.

7 Position the tail on the back of the mouse and sew it in place with a few whipstitches in pale pink sewing thread.

8 Position half of a small snap fastener with the hole to the mouse's paw, as pictured; set the other half aside to attach to the wand later. Stitch it in place with a double thickness of gray sewing thread.

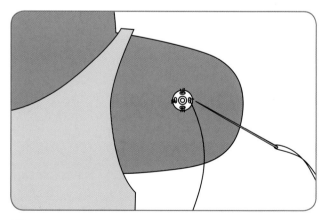

9 Trim the pieces of the mouse's top so they overlap the mouse's body by just a couple of millimeters. Place the front and back of the mouse together, wrong sides facing, and pin. Then whipstitch the front and back pieces together, starting from the mouse's shoulder and working round the arm, both legs, and then the other arm. Use matching sewing threads, changing thread colors as needed and removing the pins as you sew each section.

10 Stuff the mouse's arms, legs, and body. Add small pieces of stuffing at a time, filling the shapes firmly.

11 Pin the stitch guide to the mouse's head, and use it to mark the stitching lines on the ears with the air erasable marker. Then remove the guide.

12 Begin sewing around the head, using pins as needed to hold the front and back together. Use whipstitch and matching gray sewing thread, following the stitching line when sewing across the bottom of the ears. Stitch most of the way around the head, leaving a gap for stuffing.

13 Stuff the head firmly, then close up the remaining gap with more whipstitches.

14 Stitch the front and back of each ear together with whipstitch and matching gray sewing thread.

15 Place the two skirt pieces on top of each other and pin them together. Using whipstitch and matching lilac sewing thread, sew the two short sides together, forming a loop. Take care not to sew too tightly; you need to open out and flatten the seams afterward.

16 Add a length of silver rickrack to one edge of the felt loop; this edge will become the bottom of the skirt.

Start at what will be the back of the skirt, folding the end of the rickrack over and securing it with a few whipstitches in matching gray sewing thread. Then sew small whipstitches at intervals along one side of the rickrack to secure it. Trim the end of the rickrack to fit the remaining space, folding the end over as before. Secure it with a few whipstitches, then sew back along the other side of the rickrack.

> **TIP**
> **Complete this step as neatly as possible because the stitching will be visible inside the skirt.**

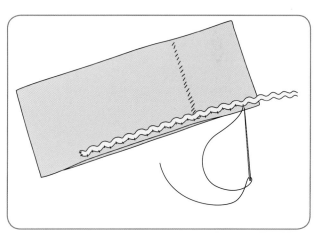

17 Sew around the top edge of the skirt with running stitch (page ix) and a long double thickness of matching lilac sewing thread. Start from the back and sew all the way round the skirt with one length of thread; this is important for the next step. Don't tie a knot yet.

18 Place the skirt around the mouse's body and carefully pull the thread so the skirt bunches up around the mouse's waist. Make sure the back of the skirt is at the back of the mouse. When the skirt has been pulled tight around the waist, secure it with a few stitches.

19 Arrange the skirt so it is evenly bunched around the waist. Then sew small whipstitches in matching thread along the top edge to secure the skirt to the top of the dress.

20 Add a line of silver sequins to the belt piece cut in step 1. Use two stitches of lilac thread per sequin, forming a stitched line down the center of the row. Leave a small gap at each end of the belt.

21 Sew the belt onto the dress, covering up the join where the skirt meets the top. Whipstitch the end in place at the back. Use matching lilac thread and a running stitch to attach it along the top edge. Then secure the second end (trimming any excess felt if necessary) and sew back along the bottom edge with more running stitches.

Make the Wings

1 Use the templates provided to cut the wing pieces from felt and the insert from white card stock. Turn one of the wing pieces over; this will be the back of the wings.

2 Decorate both wing pieces with silver sequins, sewing a line of sequins around the outside edge of both shapes. Sew each sequin in place with three stitches of pale lilac sewing thread (to match the felt) and leave room to sew the edges of the felt together later.

3 Add more sequins to the back wing piece, leaving a space in the center for adding the yarn ties in the next step.

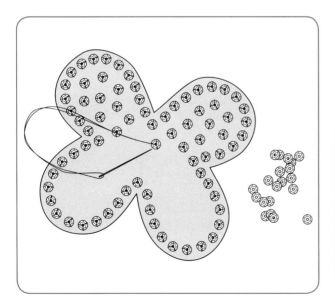

4 Turn both wing pieces over. Use a glue stick to lightly coat one side of the card stock insert with glue. Position it in the center of one of the wing pieces, and press and smooth it down onto the felt. Add more glue to the other side of the card stock and place the second felt piece on top to create a "sandwich," then press and smooth the felt so it's glued evenly.

5 Whipstitch around the edge of the wings using matching pale lilac sewing thread. Sew into the felt only, not the card stock insert.

6 Cut a length of lilac yarn measuring approximately 25 inches (63.5 cm). Thread a large, sharp needle and use it to poke two holes in the middle of the wings just over 1 inch (2.5 cm) apart. Thread the yarn through the holes to create the ties for the wings.

> **TIP**
> To attach the wings, place the mouse on top of the wings and wrap the yarn ends over the arms. Take the yarn under the arms and to the back, and tie it in a bow between the wings and the back of the mouse. Or, tie the yarn around the mouse's waist.

Make the Wand

1 Use the templates provided to cut out the star and wand pieces from felt. Turn over one of each piece; these will become the back of the wand.

2 Position both stars on their corresponding wands, and secure them with a few whipstitches in matching pink sewing thread where the star meets the wand. Then add a silver sequin to the center of each star. Sew each sequin in place with three stitches of pink thread.

3 Sew the second half of the snap fastener used earlier (in step 8) to the back wand piece, at the position marked on the template with an X. Use a double thickness of pale lilac sewing thread to match the wand.

4 Cut a length of pipe cleaner measuring just under 2 inches (5.1 cm). Sew down one side of the wand and then up the other with small whipstitches, then carefully insert the pipe cleaner into the wand, between the two layers of felt.

5 Sew around the star with whipstitch and matching pink thread. The finished wand can now be attached to the mouse's paw using the snap fastener.

FARMER HARE

DESIGNER: JESSICA FEDIW

This rabbit has a fondness for gardening. He loves to spend his days outside in his beautiful garden. He always wears his favorite pair of overalls and carries his basket when he tends to his vegetables. He takes care to make sure all of his plants have enough water and sun. He always shares the carrots and lettuce he's grown in his garden with his rabbit family and friends—so delicious!

MATERIALS

Templates (page 79–81)

Fabric for the rabbit and his shirt, ¼ yard (22.9 cm) of each fabric used

Fleece for the rabbit's overalls, ¼ yard (22.9 cm)

Light brown felt for the basket, ¼ yard (22.9 cm)

Stuffing

Leather for overall straps, 2 x 4-inch (5.1 x 10.2 cm) piece

Black embroidery floss

Glue stick

TOOLS

Fabric scissors

Straight pins

Hand-sewing needle

Iron

Embroidery needle

Turning tool, ³⁄₁₆ inch (5 mm) in diameter

Hot glue gun

NOTE
All seam allowances are ¼ inch (6 mm) unless otherwise specified.

INSTRUCTIONS

Make the Rabbit

1 Cut out a 10 x 2-inch (25.4 x 5.1 cm) piece of rabbit fabric and a 10 x 5-inch piece (25.4 x 12.7 cm) of shirt fabric. Match up the two pieces along the 10-inch (25.4 cm) side of the fabric and pin the pieces together with the right sides facing. Sew together and press the seam open. Place the arm template on top of the fabric, matching the seam line to where it is indicated on the pattern. Cut out four arm pieces.

2 Use the templates to also cut four ear pieces, one back of head piece, two front of head pieces (one facing right and one facing left), and four legs from the rabbit fabric. Cut two body pieces from the shirt fabric.

3 Pin the two ear pieces together, right sides facing. Sew them together, leaving an opening on the straight end. Cut notches on the seam allowance at the curves (see page xi). Repeat for the other ear.

4 Repeat step 3 for the legs and arms.

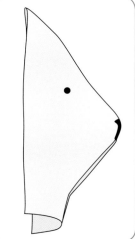

5 Place the two front head pieces together, right sides facing. Sew them together, leaving the two straight sides open. Cut notches on the seam allowance at the curves. Press the seam open.

6 Turn the legs, arms, and ears right side out. Press and then lightly stuff. Leave 1 inch (2.5 cm) empty at the opening.

7 Embroider the eyes, nose, and mouth onto the face using black embroidery floss.

8 Pin the head back to the body piece at the neckline with right sides facing. Sew them together and press the seam open.

9 Repeat step 8 to sew the front head piece to the other body piece.

10 With the ear pieces lined up at the edges, pin the ears to the top of head back piece with right sides facing. Sew them in place as close to edge as possible. Repeat for the arm pieces on either side of the body.

11 Keep the ears and arms turned inward and pin the back of the rabbit to the front piece with right sides facing. Sew them together, leaving the bottom open. Cut notches in the seam allowances on the curves. Turn right side out and stuff. Fold the bottom seam in and place the legs in. Sew across the bottom.

Make the Overalls

1 Use the templates provided to cut out two overall tops and two overall pant legs from the fleece fabric. Use the overall strap template to cut two straps from the leather.

2 With a pant leg folded with the right side facing, sew the leg together on the side opposite of fold. Repeat for the other pant leg.

3 Turn one pant leg right side out and place it inside the other pant leg. Match them up at the seam. Sew them together around the curve (crotch). Pull the legs right side out. Fold the waist edges ¼ inch (6 mm) to the wrong side and sew them in place.

4 Center and pin a top piece's bottom to the front middle waist with right sides facing. Sew together. Repeat with the other top piece on the back of the pants.

5 Sew the straps to the front side of the overalls. Crisscross the straps at the back and sew them to the back of the overalls at the bottom.

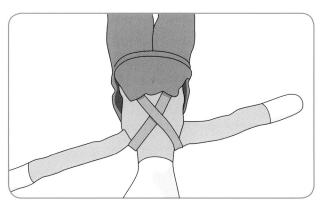

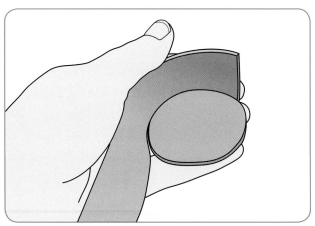

Make the Basket

Using the basket template pieces, cut out a bottom, side, and handle from the felt. Use a glue gun and glue sticks to attach the bottom piece's edges to the sides of the basket. Slowly wrap around and glue the side piece until it overlaps. Glue the side ends together at the overlap. Hand-stitch the handle onto opposite sides of the basket.

TIP
You can make veggies for your rabbit's basket out of clay. Use modeling clay in orange and green to sculpt little carrots to place in the rabbit's basket (as pictured), or use the clay to make other garden vegetables: rabbits are fond of asparagus, lettuce, and eggplant too.

FESTIVAL PANDA

DESIGNER: LAURA HOWARD

Lynne is a music-loving panda and aspiring singer-songwriter who loves spending her summers at music festivals! Come rain or shine you'll find her at a festival most summer weekends, performing her own songs or going to see her favorite bands perform. She always arrives early to make sure she and her friends can pitch their tent in the perfect spot. Lynne loves to make headbands from fresh flowers (perfect for those festival selfies!) and to accessorize with her collection of colorful jewelry. But the one thing she's never without is her guitar: it's her prized possession and she takes it everywhere, just in case song inspiration strikes. It comes in very handy in the evenings for campfire sing-alongs with all her friends.

MATERIALS

Templates (page 82–83)
White felt, one 9 x 12-inch (22.9 x 30.5 cm) sheet
Black felt, one 9 x 12-inch (22.9 x 30.5 cm) sheet
Small pieces of felt in bright colors for the flowers
Small piece of purple felt for the headband
Ginger felt, approximately 3 ½ x 6 ½ inches
    (8.9 x 16.5 cm), for the guitar
Dark brown felt, approximately 4 x 6 ½ inches
    (10.2 x 16.5 cm), for the guitar
White, black, purple, yellow, ginger,
    and dark brown sewing thread
Black stranded embroidery floss
Stuffing

Jewelry thread or elastic
Colorful seed beads
Clear adhesive tape (optional)
14 inches (61 cm) of narrow purple ribbon
Yellow seed beads
10 inches (25.4 cm) of narrow ribbon
    for the guitar strap

TOOLS

Scissors
Small, sharp embroidery scissors
Straight pins
Fine hand-sewing needle
Pencil or other narrow stuffing tool

INSTRUCTIONS

Make the Panda

1 Use the templates provided to cut out the body, ear, circle, eye, nose, tail, arm, and leg pieces from felt. Also cut out two small black circles for the pupils.

2 Arrange the black circles and white eyes on the panda's face, as pictured, and sew them in place with whipstitches (page x) and matching sewing thread. Then add the pupils and the nose with more whipstitches.

3 Cut a length of black embroidery floss and separate half the strands (so for six-stranded floss, use three strands). Use the floss to backstitch (page viii) the panda's mouth.

4 Place two of the ear shapes together and whipstitch around the curved edge with black sewing thread. Repeat to sew the second ear.

5 Place two arm shapes together and whipstitch down one side with black thread. Gradually sew up the other side of the arm, stuffing it gradually with small pieces of toy stuffing. Leave the straight end of the arm unstitched and leave about ½ inch (1.3 cm) at the top of the arm unstuffed. Repeat to sew and stuff the other arm and both legs.

6 Sew the two tail pieces together. Start at the flatter end—this will become the top of the tail—and whipstitch around the edge with white sewing thread. Leave a small gap, stuff the tail lightly, then close up the gap with more whipstitches.

7 Turn over the back body piece. Center the tail about 1½ inches from bottom edge and sew it in place with white sewing thread and a few whipstitches along the top edge.

8 Pin the front and back panda shapes together, pinning the arms and legs into the body one at a time. Start near the panda's shoulder and whipstitch down around the body with white sewing thread, sewing one arm, both legs, and then the other arm. Remove the pins when you come to them, as they are no longer needed.

9 Stuff the body gradually, adding small pieces until it's firmly filled.

10 Pin the panda's head together, with the ears inserted at the top. Begin sewing around the head with whipstitch and white thread, removing the pins when you come to them, as they are no longer needed.

11 Stuff the panda's head firmly, adding small pieces of toy stuffing at a time. Sew up the remaining gap with more whipstitches and white thread.

Make the Necklaces

1 Cut a 16-inch (40.6 cm) length of strong white thread or narrow jewelry elastic. Thread a fine needle and string lots of seed beads onto the thread/elastic.

2 Continue adding beads until they measure 9 to 10 inches (22.9 to 254 cm), then tie the ends of the thread/elastic together, knotting it securely. Trim the excess thread.

3 Repeat steps 1 and 2 to make several necklaces in slightly different lengths and different colors.

Make the Flower Headband

1 Use the templates provided to cut out the headband and flower pieces from felt.

2 Cut a piece of narrow purple ribbon measuring approximately 14 inches (35.6 cm). Position the ribbon so it's centered on one of the headband pieces, as pictured. Sew the ribbon and felt together with running stitch (page ix) and matching sewing thread.

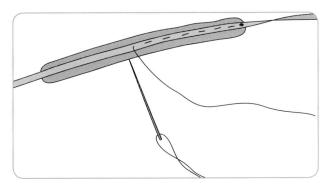

3 Turn the headband piece over so the ribbon is underneath it. Sew the flowers along the top, one by one. Start in the center of the headband, sewing the flowers so they slightly overlap each other. Use a double thickness of yellow sewing thread and a couple of very small stitches per flower.

4 Add one yellow seed bead to the center of each flower, sewing them in place with a double thickness of yellow thread.

5 Turn the headband over and place the two long headband pieces together. Use matching sewing thread and whipstitches to join the edges of the headband pieces together, taking care to pull the flowers back to avoid stitching into them.

> **TIP**
> **When tying the headband around the panda's head for the first time, trim the ribbon, if needed. Cut the ends at an angle to help prevent fraying.**

Make the Guitar

1 Use the templates provided to cut out the guitar pieces from felt.

2 Sew the neck of the guitar, the sound hole, and the bridge onto the ginger guitar shape, as pictured, with whipstitch and matching thread. Only sew the bottom of the guitar's neck to the backing felt, leaving the outside edges of the guitar unstitched.

3 Add five strings to the guitar, running from the bridge to the head of the guitar, as pictured. Make each string from one long stitch of white sewing thread, knotting the thread after each stitch to help keep it tight. Start with the middle string, then add the outer ones, spacing them evenly.

4 Cut a 10-inch (25.4 cm) piece of narrow ribbon for the guitar strap. Attach the ends of the ribbon to the back (dark brown) guitar shape, as pictured, so that the ribbon is not twisted and the ends will be hidden inside the guitar when it's finished. Use whipstitch and dark brown sewing thread, sewing into the felt, not through it, so the stitching will be hidden.

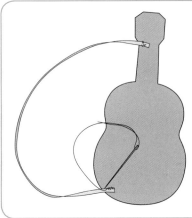

5 Pin the front and back guitar pieces together at the neck. Sew the neck together with matching dark brown thread and whipstitches, then remove the pins.

6 Stuff the neck with very small pieces of toy stuffing and a pencil or other narrow stuffing tool.

7 Begin sewing around the rest of the guitar with whipstitches and matching ginger sewing thread. Start at the bottom of the guitar and sew up to the neck. Finish and then restart stitching on either side of the neck—don't sew across it! Continue stitching, leaving a gap at the bottom of the guitar for stuffing.

8 Stuff the guitar lightly with small pieces of stuffing; take care not to overstuff it and distort the shape. Then sew up the gap with more whipstitches.

HERBERT THE ARTIST FROG

DESIGNER: MOLLIE JOHANSON

When Herbert was just a froglet, he went to the museum and saw some beautiful paintings of water lilies. They reminded him of the pond where he lived, and right then and there he decided to become an artist. Now he paints trees, water, grapes, cardinals, marigolds, bees, and more. All the colors of the rainbow! Give him a brush and you might just see him paint a masterpiece.

MATERIALS

Templates (page 84–86)
Lime green fleece, ¼ yard (22.9 cm)
Black felt, 9 x 12 inches (22.9 x 30.5 cm)
White felt, 8 x 5 ½ inches (20.3 x 14 cm)
Tan felt, 4 ½ x 7 inches (11.4 x 17.8 cm)
Felt scraps in rainbow colors
Red felt scrap
Sewing thread in coordinating colors
Red, black, and tan embroidery floss
Two 12 mm safety eyes
Stuffing
24 inches (61 cm) of black ribbon, ¾ inch (1.9 cm) wide
Fabric glue
3-inch (7.6 cm) piece of wide elastic (fold-over elastic works well)

TOOLS

Scissors
Erasable fabric pen
Embroidery needle
Straight pins
Sewing machine
Hand-sewing needle

> **NOTE**
> All seam allowances are ¼ inch (6 mm).

INSTRUCTIONS

Make the Frog

1. Cut two body pieces from fleece and transfer the markings for the face onto one piece. Cut four arm pieces and four leg pieces from fleece. Cut one tongue piece from red felt. Be sure to follow the stretch markings on the fleece pieces.

2. On the front body piece, cut two tiny holes where the eyes will go and install the safety eyes. (If you will be giving this to a young child, embroider or appliqué the eyes instead.) Appliqué the felt tongue in place using whipstitch (page x) and red embroidery floss. Embroider the mouth using backstitch (page viii) and black embroidery floss.

3. Pin two arm pieces with wrong sides together and sew around the sides and bottom, leaving the straight, non-flared edge open for stuffing. Repeat with the other arm and leg pieces, and then add stuffing. The raw edges will remain on the outside.

4. Place the back body piece wrong side up, then lay the arms and legs on top, with the straight edges facing in and overlapping about ½ inch (1.3 cm). Baste the pieces in place.

5. Pin the front body piece to the back with wrong sides together. Sew around the sides, leaving an opening for stuffing. Clip the curves (see page xi). Stuff the body, and sew the opening closed.

Make the Beret

Cut two hat pieces from black felt and cut the center oval out from one of them. Stitch around the outside with running stitch (page ix). Cut a rectangular scrap of the black felt approximately ½-inch wide and ¾-inch long. Sew the bottom of the rectangular tab to the top of the beret using whipstitch.

Make the Smock

With the white felt rectangle lying horizontally, mark and cut two 1½-inch (3.8 cm) slits for Herbert's arms. The slits should be 2 inches (5.1 cm) in from the sides, and ¾ inch (1.9 cm) from the top. Center the black ribbon across the smock and stitch along the top edge with two rows of running stitch.

Make the Palette

Cut two palette pieces from tan felt. Cut six paint circles from scraps of rainbow colors of felt. Glue the paint dots to the front of one of the palette pieces. Sew the elastic to the back palette piece on the right side; leave some slack so there's room for Herbert's hand to slip through. Stitch the two palette pieces together with running stitch using the tan embroidery floss.

JAMES THE KING OF THE JUNGLE

DESIGNER: MOLLIE JOHANSON

James is just a little lion with a mane that isn't quite fully grown yet. He's still a bit timid, and that's what makes him sweet and lovable. James dreams of growing up to be the king of the jungle, but for now he's happy to dress up in a crown and cape. Best of all, the cape makes a nice blankie for him to snuggle with.

MATERIALS

Templates (page 87–89)

Light yellow fleece, ¼ yard (22.9 cm)

Orange felt, 4 x 6 inches (10.2 x 15.2 cm)

Black felt scrap

Golden yellow felt, 3 x 4 inches (7.6 x 10.2 cm)

Burgundy felt, 4 ½ x 8 inches (11.4 x 20.3 cm)

White felt, 6 x 17 inches (15.2 x 43.2 cm)

Sewing thread in coordinating colors

Black, white, and golden yellow embroidery floss

Two 9 mm safety eyes

Stuffing

Fabric glue

1-inch (2.5 cm) strip of hook-and-loop fastener

TOOLS

Scissors

Erasable marking pen

Embroidery needle

Straight pins

Sewing machine

Turning tool

Hand-sewing needle

> **NOTE**
> All seam allowances are ¼ inch (6 mm).

INSTRUCTIONS

Make the Lion

1 Cut two body pieces from fleece and transfer the markings for the face onto one piece. Cut four ear pieces and four arm pieces from fleece. Cut one mane piece from orange felt, and cut one nose piece from black felt. Be sure to follow the stretch markings on the fleece pieces (see page xi).

2 On the front body piece, cut two tiny holes where the eyes will go and install the safety eyes. (If you will be giving this to a young child, embroider or appliqué the eyes instead.) Appliqué the mane and nose in place with whipstitch (page x), and embroider the mouth using backstitch (page viii).

3 Pin two ear pieces with right sides together and sew around the curved edge, leaving the straight edge open for turning. Repeat with the other ear and arm pieces. Turn the pieces right side out and stuff the arms.

4 Place the back body piece right side up, then lay the ears and arms on top, with raw edges aligned and the finished sides facing in. Baste the pieces in place.

5 Pin the front body piece to the back with right sides together. Sew around the sides, leaving an opening for turning. Clip the curves (see page xi), then turn the body right side out.

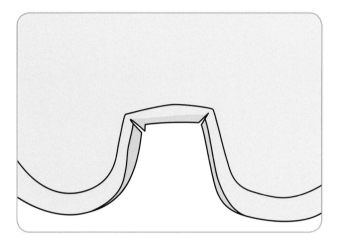

6 Stuff the body and sew the opening closed with ladder stitch (page ix).

Make the Crown

Cut two crown pieces from golden yellow felt and stitch the sides with running stitch (page ix) and golden yellow embroidery floss.

Make the Cape

1 Cut two capes pieces from burgundy felt, and two 1³/₄ x 17-inch (4.4 x 43.2 cm) rectangles and two 1³/₄ x 8 ¹/₂-inch (4.4 x 21.6 cm) rectangles from white felt. Round the corners on the white rectangles. On one long and one short rectangle, stitch short running stitches with black embroidery floss.

2 Sandwich the wider edge of the cape piece between the two short rectangles and stitch around the white rectangles with running stitch and white embroidery floss. Repeat with the long rectangles at the top edge of the cape. Wrap the long strips around James and glue the hook-and-loop fastener in place where the strips overlap.

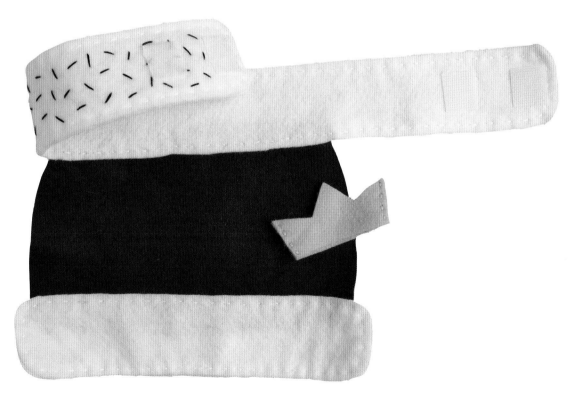

MINDY THE SWIMMING MONKEY

DESIGNER: MOLLIE JOHANSON

Splash! Some monkeys like swinging from the trees, but Mindy would rather dive in the pool for some exercise! After she swims a few laps and is starting to feel tired, Mindy hops into her swim ring and floats around the pool before climbing out and toweling off. Some days, if she's not up for getting all wet, she lies out in the sun to maintain her beautiful brown tan. It's a good thing monkeys don't need sunscreen!

MATERIALS

Templates (page 90–92)
Brown fleece, ¼ yard (22.9 cm)
Tan felt scraps
Pink felt, 7 x 9 inches (17.8 x 22.9 cm)
2 pieces of teal felt, 10 x 10 inches
    (25.4 x 25.4 cm) each
Yellow felt, 5 x 5 inches (12.7 x 12.7 cm)
White terry cloth or half a washcloth,
    5 x 11 inches (12.7 x 27.9 cm)
Sewing threads
Brown, pink, and yellow embroidery floss
Two 12 mm safety eyes
Stuffing
1 yard (91.4 cm) of yellow ribbon, ½ inch
    (1.3 cm) wide
Fabric glue

TOOLS

Scissors
Erasable marking pen
Embroidery needle
Straight pins
Sewing machine
Hand-sewing needle

NOTE
All seam allowances are ¼ inch (6 mm).

INSTRUCTIONS

Make the Monkey

1 Cut two body pieces from fleece and transfer the markings for the face onto one piece. Cut four arm pieces, four leg pieces, and two tail pieces from fleece. Be sure to follow the stretch markings on the fleece pieces (see page xi). Cut two ear pieces and one muzzle piece from the scraps of tan felt.

2 On the front body piece, cut two tiny holes where the eyes will go and install the safety eyes. (If you will be giving this to a young child, embroider or appliqué the eyes instead.) Embroider the mouth with backstitch (page viii) on the muzzle and stitch the muzzle to the front body piece with running stitch (page ix) using brown embroidery floss.

3 Pin two arm pieces with wrong sides together and sew around the sides and bottom, leaving the straight edge open for stuffing. Repeat with the other arm pieces. Do the same with the leg and tail pieces. Add stuffing to the arm and leg pieces. The raw edges will remain on the outside.

4 Sew the tail on the back body piece, as marked on the template. Place the back body piece wrong side up, then lay the ears, arms, and legs on top, with the straight edges facing in and overlapping about ½ inch (1.3 cm). Baste the pieces in place.

5 Pin the front body piece to the back with wrong sides together, and pin the tail up so it isn't in the way. Sew around the sides, leaving an opening for turning. Clip the curves (see page xi). Turn the piece right side out, stuff body and sew the opening closed with ladder stitch (page ix).

Make the Bikini

Cut a 1½ x 5½-inch (3.8 x 14 cm) rectangle and two bikini bottom pieces from pink felt. Stitch a line of running stitch in the middle of the rectangle with matching thread and pull gently to gather the center before tying off with a knot. Cut the ribbon into four 9-inch (22.9 cm) pieces and stitch one piece to each corner of the rectangle at a slight angle. Cut a slit for Mindy's tail in one of the bikini bottom pieces and stitch an X at each end to prevent stretching. Stitch the two bottom pieces together on the sides and bottom using running stitch.

Make the Swim Ring

Cut two swim ring pieces on the fold from teal felt. Cut seven banana shapes from the yellow felt using the template provided. Use fabric glue to attach the banana pieces to one of the swim ring pieces. After the glue has dried, pin the swim ring pieces together and stitch around the center circle with running stitch. Begin stitching around the outside circle with running stitch. Halfway around, add stuffing to the section that is sewn. Continue stitching and adding stuffing until the entire tube is stuffed and stitched.

Make the Towel

Use pink embroidery floss to stitch a border of blanket stitch (page viii) around the terry cloth piece. Stitch with care, as terry cloth can snag. If it does, simply trim away with threads without cutting the embroidery floss.

MOD CHICK

DESIGNER: SUZIE MILLIONS

Petula Lark is a happy little mod chick, ready to sing a sweet song and look smashing while she's doing it in her happening go-go boots, groovy poncho, and fabulous cap. She loves to sing and dance along to her favorite tunes with her birdy friends. When she's not busy grooving at a hip and happening bash, Petula likes to perch atop high-up places for some rest and relaxation.

MATERIALS

Templates (page 93–95)

Blue burlap, 1/3 yard (30.5 cm)

Patterned cotton for belly, legs, and beak, 1/3 yard (30.5 cm)

Colorful cotton for poncho and cap, 1/3 yard (30.5 cm)

Blue felt, 9 x 12 inches (22.9 x 30.5 cm)

White stiffened felt, 4 x 4 inches (10.2 x 10.2 cm)

White vinyl with backing, 12 x 4 inches (30.5 x 10.2 cm)

Trim for poncho collar, 18 inches (45.7 cm)

3/8-inch (9.5 mm) pompom trim, 30 inches (76.2 cm)

Sewing thread to match patterned cotton, to match trim, and in blue

Black upholstery thread

Double-sided transparent tape (see Tip below)

White glue

Jumbo glue stick

Stuffing

2 black buttons for eyes, 7/16 inch (1.1 cm) in diameter

Decorative button for poncho

2 small buttons for the cap

Gold trim for the cap

TOOLS

Scissors

Small paintbrush

Straight pins

Heavy-duty hand-sewing needle

Turning tool or wooden dowel, 3/8 inch (9.5 mm) in diameter

2 ball-head straight pins

Craft knife (if using shank buttons for eyes)

Iron

Rotary cutter and self-healing mat (optional)

> **TIP**
> Use double-sided transparent tape to attach templates for small items to fabric.

INSTRUCTIONS
Make the Chick

1 Use the template to cut two body pieces from blue burlap. With one piece facing right and one piece facing left, brush a 1/8-inch (3 mm) strip all along the edge with white glue to minimize fraying. Set aside to dry.

2 Cut two rectangles measuring 9 x 6 inches (22.9 x 15.25 cm) from the patterned cotton and blue felt. This will be for the belly and beak. Apply the glue stick to the back of patterned cotton. Press it down onto the piece of blue felt. Set aside.

3 Use the template to cut two legs from the patterned cotton: fold 2 inches (5.1 cm) of the fabric over with right sides facing, place the long straight edge of the leg template on the fold, pin, and cut; repeat for the other leg. Remove the template and repin each leg, keeping right sides together. Use a running stitch (page ix) to first close the foot (the curved end) and then the open side of the leg. Leave the top open.

4 Use a turning tool to turn the legs right side out. (If you don't have one, use a wooden dowel to gently push the toe through the leg to reverse it.) Push a ball-head pin into the edge of the seam so the head is resting 2 1/2 inches (6.4 cm) down from the top of the leg.

5 Fill the legs with small pieces of stuffing, using the turning tool or dowel to push it into the foot and leg, stopping at the pin head; the stuffing should be firm but not packed to the point it stresses the seams. At the pin marking, make small, close running stitches all the way across the leg to form the knee. Add fill above the knee, and then close the top edge of the leg with a blanket stitch (page viii).

6 Pin the body pieces together, unglued sides facing. Put a ball-head pin at the starting and stopping point for stitching, as indicated on the template. Stitching in the unglued burlap just beyond the glued edge, use a small running stitch to sew from the starting point below the tail, up over the back to the ending point below the beak. Turn right side out. Run a finger along the inside of the seams to open them up.

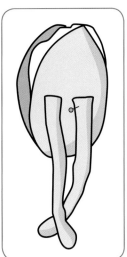

7 Use the template to cut the belly from the patterned cotton mounted on felt. Pin it on the body, overlapping the opening 1/2 inch (1.3 cm) at the top and 1/4 inch (6 mm) on the sides; leave the back third open. Whipstitch (page x) the belly in place, still leaving the back third open.

8 Fill the body with small pieces of stuffing.

9 Pin the legs to the belly panel with their top edge facing the back of the chick, 2 1/2 inches (6.4 cm) down from the end of the belly panel, side seams facing the inside, and the legs 1/2 inch (1.3 cm) apart.

10 On each leg, start on the outside of the top edge and whipstitch it to the inside of that edge, turn the corner and whipstitch 1/2 inch (1.3 cm) down the inside edge, and then turn the corner and make a running stitch all the way across the leg, taking each stitch through both the leg and belly panel, keeping one hand on the underside of the panel to pull the needle all the way through and then return it to the outside. Leave the side of the leg that faces out unstitched. Close the belly with a whipstitch.

11 Use the template to cut the beak from a scrap of patterned cotton mounted on felt. Position it on the chick and hold it in place with two straight pins. Make several stitches to tack one end in place, then whipstitch under the beak to attach it to the chick, passing the needle through the beak's felt backing but not through the cotton on top. Tack the other end of the beak in place with several stitches.

12 Use the template to cut the wings from the blue felt. Position them on the chick (see page 114) and hold in place with pins. Sew them in place using whipstitch along the top portion of the wings, leaving the bottom free.

13 Use the template to cut two eyes from the stiffened white felt. Sew a black button in the center of each. If the buttons have a shank, cut a tiny X in the center of the white circles and press the shank through it before stitching. With the thread still attached to the back of the circle, stitch the eyes onto the chick.

Make the Go-Go Boots

Using the templates, cut two boots from white vinyl. All the seams on the boot are sewn on the outside using a whipstitch and black upholstery thread. Start the needle on the inside of the toe, continue up the foot to the leg, and finish at the top of the boot, knotting the thread on the inside of the boot before clipping. Starting on an outside edge, stitch the sole to the back panels, with one panel slightly overlapping the other. After the last stitch on the sole, move the needle to the bottom of the back panel seam through the inside of the boot and stitch up to the top of the boot, knotting off the thread on the inside before clipping.

Make the Poncho

1 Fold the colorful cotton so that the poncho template can be used to cut out two pieces at once, placing one edge on the fold. Press the folded side flat. Use the template to cut out a poncho. (If you have a rotary cutter, this is a good use for it.)

2 With the template still in place, fold the poncho in half and cut the circle opening out of the middle of it. Brush the edges of the opening and the hem with white glue to prevent fraying, if necessary.

3 Stitch the trim around the poncho collar. Pin the pompom trim on the hem of one side of the poncho and whipstitch it in place from the back (the side without the collar trim); be sure both layers of cotton are being stitched. Turn the pompom trim on the corner and use the pins from the last side sewn to pin it in place on the next side. On the corner, double-stitch and knot the thread but don't cut it; continue sewing and turning until all four sides of the poncho hem are trimmed. The poncho is worn with a point in the center.

4 Pick the best-looking side and sew a decorative button on it as pictured.

Make the Cap

1 Use the cap template to cut a circle from the colorful cotton.

2 Use the templates to cut the cap crown and inner ring from the white stiffened felt. Overlap the ends of the inner ring and stitch a couple times to close it.

3 Baste 1/8 inch (3 mm) from the edge all around the circle of fabric for the cap, leaving 2 inches (5.1 cm) of thread to pull at both the starting and the stopping point.

4 Put the circle right side down on the work surface. Put the cap crown in the center of it and then the inner ring, curved edge down, with the overlapping seam next to the thread ends. Pull the threads and gather the fabric around the inner ring. Once the fabric is snug around the inner ring and the gathers are even, tie the pull threads together.

5 Use the template to cut the cap brim from white vinyl. Position the inside edge of it on the inside of the assembled cap, with the center of the brim opposite the overlapping seam on the inner ring. Whipstitch it in place on the underside, catching the backing on the vinyl but avoiding stitching through the vinyl. On the top side, stitch the gold trim in place where the brim meets the top of the cap. Sew a tiny button to cover the end of the trim on both sides.

OWL AND PUSSYCAT

DESIGNER: AIMEE RAY

Kitty is ready for bed with his little toy owl friend! He likes to dream up fantastical fairy tales before bedtime and always reads his favorite book before falling peacefully asleep. With his fluffy cloud pillow, cozy blanket, and owl by his side, Kitty can't help but sleep well. Tuck him in with his nightshirt, blanket, cloud pillow, and a book to read.

MATERIALS

Templates (page 96)

Felt in blue, light gray, dark gray, white, purple, and aqua, each 9 x 12 inches (22.9 x 30.5 cm)

2 pieces of blue-and-white striped fabric for the mattress, each 7 x 9 inches (17.8 x 22.9 cm)

2 pieces of white fabric for the blanket, each 10 x 2 inches (25.4 x 5.1 cm)

2 pieces of blue star fabric for the blanket, each 10 x 6 inches (25.4 x 15.2 cm)

Matching threads (Note: Instead of buying thread to match each color of felt, you can use two threads from a strand of matching embroidery floss for hand-sewing.)

Embroidery floss in light gray, dark gray, blue, and dark brown

Stuffing

Pink chalk pastel (optional)

TOOLS

Straight pins

Fabric scissors

Hand-sewing needle

Embroidery needle

Soft paintbrush or cotton swab (optional)

Sewing machine

Iron

INSTRUCTIONS

> **NOTE**
> To begin, pin each of the paper templates to the felt and cut each piece out.

Make the Kitty

1 Pin the two kitty body parts together and whipstitch (page x) them around the edges, inserting some stuffing inside.

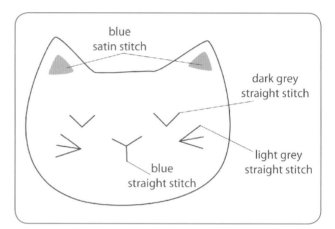

2 For the kitty's head, first embroider the face according to the pattern. You can add some blush to kitty's cheeks with chalk pastels on a soft brush or cotton swab, if desired.

3 Pin the front and back of the head together and sew around the edges using the whipstitch. Leave the bottom open and tuck some stuffing inside, then fit the hole over the neck of the body and sew it on securely.

Make the Book

For the book, line up the white page piece inside the purple cover piece and fold them in half. Make a line of backstitches (page viii) along the folded edge of the book. Appliqué the moon on the cover using the stab stitch (page ix).

Make the Pillow

Pin the two cloud pillow parts together and whipstitch them around the edges, inserting some stuffing inside.

Make the Nightshirt

Pin the front and back nightshirt pieces together and sew the shoulder sections and underarm sections together using the whipstitch. Sew a felt button on the front as pictured. Fit the nightshirt over kitty's arms with the opening at the back.

Make the Owl

For the owl, sew the eye piece and belly piece in place on one body piece using the stab stitch. Embroider the eye, beak, and feather details. Pin the front and back of the body together with a wing tucked in between at either side. Sew around the edges using the whipstitch, inserting some stuffing inside.

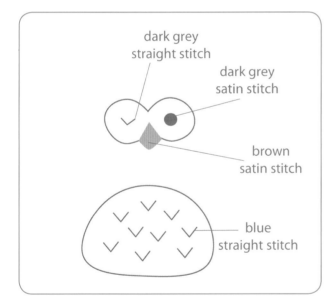

dark grey
straight stitch

dark grey
satin stitch

brown
satin stitch

blue
straight stitch

Make the Blanket

For the blanket, sew a white strip along the top edge of each 10 x 6-inch (25.4 x 15.2 cm) piece of star fabric. Pin the pieces together with right sides facing and sew around the edges with a sewing machine, leaving 1 inch (2.5 cm) open at the end. Turn the blanket right side out and press the seams. Topstitch (page ix) 1/4 inch (6 mm) in from the edge around the sides of the blanket.

Make the Mattress

For the mattress, pin the front and back pieces together with right sides facing and sew around the edges with a sewing machine, leaving 1 inch (2.5 cm) open at the end. Turn the mattress right side out and fill it with stuffing. Stitch up the opening.

PARTY FOX

DESIGNER: JESSICA FEDIW

This party fox just loves to dress up to go to parties. She likes to dance (her favorite dance is called the foxtrot!), and she especially loves when there are photo booths at parties. She and her friends pack themselves in to the booth and take tons of funny photo-booth photos. She likes to make silly faces and will use every prop she can! She collects all of her photo booth pictures in a special album.

MATERIALS

Templates (page 97–98)

Cotton fabric in orange, white, light green and polka-dot pattern for the fox body, head, face, and legs, and green plaid for the skirt, ¼ yard (22.9 cm) each

Felt, 2 x 2-inch square in white for the fox's collar

Matching threads

Embroidery floss for the eyes, nose, mouth, and buttons

Iron-on adhesive

Stuffing

7 inches (17.8 cm) of elastic, ¼-inch (6 mm) wide

Stiffened felt, one sheet in black

Paper straw

Box large enough to fit the fox (approximately 8 x 10 inches [20.3 x 24.4 cm])

Paper, streamers, wooden craft sticks, and other decorations for the party box

TOOLS

Fabric scissors

Sewing machine

Iron

Pencil or erasable fabric marker

Embroidery needle

Turning tool, ³⁄₁₆ inch (5 mm) in diameter

Straight pins

Hand-sewing needle

Safety pin

Paper or craft scissors

NOTE
All seam allowances are ¼ inch (6 mm) unless otherwise specified.

INSTRUCTIONS

Make the Fox

1 Cut a 10 x 4-inch (25.4 x 10.2 cm) piece of body fabric and a 10 x 4-inch (25.4 x 10.2 cm) piece of fox fabric. Match the two pieces along the 10-inch (25.4 cm) side and pin the pieces together, right sides facing. Sew them together and press open

POLAR PRINCESS

DESIGNER: SUZIE MILLIONS

This itty-bitty perma-frost princess comes with her own igloo carrying case and bejeweled robe and crown. It's chilly in the North Pole, but with her thick fur, fancy robe, and cozy igloo, this polar bear princess stays nice and warm. She loves to play in the snow with her friends. They make huge snow piles and have a blast sliding down them. Afterward, when the princess is tired from all of the fun, she goes back into her igloo to curl up for a cozy nap.

MATERIALS

Templates (page 99)

White fake fur fabric, 3 x 4-inch (7.6 x 10.2 cm) piece with the fur running the direction of the shorter edge (Note: The project pictured used 4-inch-wide [10.2 cm] fabric trim with iridescent threads)

White felt, 6 x 6 inches (15.2 x 15.2 cm)

White fleece, ½ yard (45.7 cm) plus a 5 x 2 ½-inch (12.7 x 6.4 cm) piece

White and gold sewing thread

Black upholstery thread

Double-sided tape (see Tip, below)

1 mushroom-cap black button (round on top, flat on bottom) for the nose, 7⁄16 inch (1.1 cm) in diameter

2 round black buttons for eyes, 3⁄16 inch (5 mm) in diameter

Stick-on gems, 1 packet

2½ inches (6.4 cm) of gold trim for the crown, ½-inch (1.3 cm) wide

7 inches (17.8 cm) of gold trim for the robe, ¼-inch (6 mm) wide

5 inches (12.7) of elasticized tulle trim for the robe, 1¼-inches (3.2 cm) wide

12-ounce frozen topping container, approximately 5-inch (12.7 cm) base and 4 inches (10.2 cm) tall

12 inches (30.5 cm) of elastic, ¼ inch (6 mm) wide

12 inches (30.5 cm) of decorative trim for the handle

2 icy-looking clear buttons

TOOLS

Fabric scissors

Heavy-duty hand-sewing needle

Medium-point permanent marker

Straight pins

Paper or craft scissors

Ruler or measuring tape (optional)

Piece of string (optional)

1 large safety pin

1 small safety pin

TIP

Use double-sided tape to attach small templates to fabric. For felt pieces, attach the tape to the template first and then tap it a few times on a felt scrap to make the adhesive a little less aggressive before putting it on the felt to be cut.

INSTRUCTIONS

Make the Princess

1 Use the template to cut one body piece from the white fake fur fabric. Using the sewing needle, poke holes in the center of the dots marking the ears, nose, and eyes on the body template. Put the punctured template on the back of the fur fabric and use the permanent marker to make a dot on the fabric back for each of the markings.

2 Use white thread to sew on the buttons for the nose and eyes, starting the needle on the markings on the back side of the fur fabric.

3 Use the template to cut two ears from white felt. Pinch the two sides of the base of an ear together and makes a couple of stitches to give it depth. With the thread still attached to the ear, insert the needle from the front of the fur fabric to the back, making sure the needle is in the center of the ear marking before pulling it all the way through. Make a few stitches to attach the ear. Repeat with the other ear.

4 With the fur side in, match up the two 3-inch (7.6 cm) edges of the body and whipstitch (page x) them together with thread, making stitches ⅛ inch (3 mm) in from the edge of the fabric and ⅛ inch (3 mm) apart. Lock the end of that seam with a couple of knots.

5 Make loose running stitches (page ix) along the open seam on the top edge of the body. Pull tightly after each stitch to gather the fur fabric. Stop at the end of the open seam, pull one last time to gather the fabric, and lock the stitches with a couple of knots. Turn right side out.

6 Use the template to cut two arms from white felt. Fold one arm piece in half, matching one curved edge to the other, and whipstitch the open edges, starting on the curve that will form the paw and stitching down the open side. Leave the bottom edge open. Turn right side out. Repeat to make the other arm.

7 To make the claws, thread the needle with 14 inches (35.6 cm) of black upholstery thread. Make a tight knot about 1 inch (2.5 cm) from the end of the thread. Trim the tail of thread behind the knot to ¼ inch (6 mm). Pull the needle through the curved edge of the paw from the front side to the back. Pull the knot snug against the felt without pulling it through. Return the needle from the inside of the paw to the outside, making the stitch ⅛ inch (3 mm) from the last. Pull all the thread to the outside. Make a knot at the bottom of what will be a claw by catching a small bit of felt at the base of the thread, pulling the thread through to make a very small loop, then pulling the needle through the loop and tugging it tight. Clip the thread, leaving a ¼-inch (6 mm) tail. Repeat to make one more set of claws for that paw.

8 Repeat step 7 to make two sets of claws for the other paw.

9 Open the arms up a little and pin them to the side of the body. Use white thread to whipstitch them to the body, seam side down.

10 Roll the 5 x 2½-inch (12.7 x 6.4 cm) piece of fleece along its length and the fold in half. Stuff it inside the Polar Princess's body, unfolded ends in first. Arrange the fleece to make her stand evenly.

Make the Crown

Overlap the ends of the 2½-inch (6.4 cm) piece of ½-inch (1.3 cm) gold trim and stitch them together with gold thread. Press on some stick-on gems.

Make the Robe

Overlap the ends of the 7-inch (17.8 cm) piece of ¼-inch (6 mm) gold trim and stitch them together with gold thread to make the collar. Stitch the elasticized tulle under the collar, with the collar seam in the center of the back. Press on a few stick-on gems.

Make the Igloo Bag

1 Line up the bottom of the doorway template with the top edge of the plastic container, straight edges matching, and trace with the permanent marker. Cut out with sturdy scissors.

2 Cut an 18-inch (45.7 cm) circle of white fleece; it doesn't need to be precise.

> **TIP**
>
> To make a large fabric circle, cut a square of fabric measuring the same size as the diameter of the circle being made. Fold the fabric into quarters. Lay a ruler or measuring tape diagonally from the folded corner with no open fabric edges across to the corner opposite it. Measure out the radius (the desired diameter of the circle divided by two) from the folded corner and mark with a pin. Tie a string to a marker. Holding the marker point upright on the pin, pull the string out tight and pin it to the folded corner. Swing the marker across the fabric and make an arc. Cut along the arc through all four layers to make the oversize circle.

3 Fold the fabric edge from the front side to the back ¾ inch (1.9 cm) and whipstitch to make a casing for the elastic. Stop 1 inch (2.5 cm) before reaching the starting point.

4 Put the plastic container in the center of the back side of the fleece, open end up.

5 Attach the large safety pin to one end of the elastic. Attach the small safety pin to the other end of the elastic, and then pin that end to the unsewn gap in the casing. Feed the elastic through the casing using the large pin to push it through, making gathers and pushing them back off the pin until the pin travels all the way through the casing and emerges next to the starting point.

6 Remove the safety pins and, holding the elastic ends snugly, spread the gathers evenly and adjust to make a 2-inch (5.1 cm) opening. Overlap the elastic and sew together. Trim the excess. Stitch the elastic casing closed.

7 With the opening for the igloo door facing forward, stitch the decorative trim for the handle on either side of the opening, attaching it to the bag just below the elastic casing.

8 Cover each point where the handle attaches to the bag with an icy-looking button.

> **TIP**
>
> To convert the Polar Princess's bag into an igloo, remove the princess and her accessories, push the handle and the top of the bag up into the top of the igloo, and flip it over. Pull the fleece out a bit over the door opening to make a little overhang.

SUPERHERO PIG

DESIGNER: LAURA HOWARD

By day, Samuel is an ordinary business pig, but by night (and on weekends) he's a crime-fighting superhero! He first discovered his superhero calling when his neighbor (an overly ambitious cat by the name of Maurice) got stuck in a tree. Since then, doing good has become his secret hobby. His neighborhood is quite quiet (no bank robberies to foil!), so he spends a happy few hours each evening chasing away teens spraying graffiti in the park, helping elderly animals cross the road, and replacing lightbulbs on broken streetlamps to make sure everyone gets home safe at night. His mask keeps him from being recognized by his neighbors, and his cape keeps him warm during the cold nights patrolling the streets (he also thinks it looks pretty cool).

MATERIALS

Templates (page 100–101)
Pink felt, two 9 x 12-inch (22.9 x 30.5 cm) sheets
Turquoise blue felt, one 9 x 12-inch (22.9 x 30.5 cm) sheet
Aqua blue felt, one 9 x 12-inch (22.9 x 30.5 cm) sheet
White felt, approximately 3½ x 4 inches (8.9 x 10.2 cm)
Small pieces of bright pink, pale pink, and black felt
Pink, turquoise, aqua blue, white, bright pink, pale pink, and black sewing thread
Black, pale pink, and candy pink stranded embroidery floss
Stuffing
Turquoise yarn

TOOLS

Scissors
Straight pins
Hand-sewing needle
Small, sharp embroidery scissors (optional)
Embroidery needle
Air erasable fabric marker
Large, sharp needle

INTRUCTIONS

Make the Pig

1 Use the templates provided to cut out the pig body, costume, ear, eye, nose, circle, and star pieces from felt.

2 Turn over one pig shape and one costume shape; these will become the back of the pig. Place the front costume shape on the front body shape, and pin it in position. Sew the costume onto the body with whipstitch (page x) and matching turquoise sewing thread, leaving the outside edges unstitched and removing the pins when they are no longer needed. Repeat for the back costume and body shape, then set this aside.

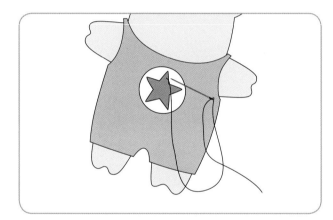

3 Sew a circle and star to the front of the costume, as pictured, using whipstitch and matching sewing threads.

4 Pin one of the mask shapes (or the mask template) to the pig's face, using it as a guide for positioning the pig's eyes. Use white sewing thread to sew a small X (made from two small single stitches) in the center of each eye, holding them in place, then remove the mask.

5 Turn over one of the ear pieces; this will be stitched to the left ear. Use whipstitch and matching threads to sew the eyes and both ear shapes in place. Then cut two small circles from black felt for the pupils and sew these in the center of the eyes with black thread and whipstitches.

TIP

To cut small felt circles, cut a small square of felt in a spiral motion, turning the felt while cutting to create a circle. Small, sharp embroidery scissors are perfect for cutting out little shapes like this.

6 Place all the nose pieces on top of each other to create the 3-D nose. Then sew them onto the pig's face with whipstitch and matching pink sewing thread.

7 Cut a length of pale pink embroidery floss and separate half the strands (i.e., for six-stranded floss, use three strands). Use this to sew two small, vertical stitches on the nose to create the nostrils.

8 Cut a length of black embroidery floss and separate half the strands. Draw the pig's smile with an air erasable fabric marker, then backstitch (page viii) the smile with the black floss.

9 Cut a length of candy pink embroidery floss and separate half the strands. Use the air erasable pen to draw a curly tail on the back of the pig then backstitch the tail with the pink floss.

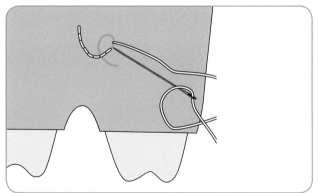

10 Trim the costume so it overlaps the pig's body by just a couple of millimeters. Place the front and back of the pig together, wrong sides facing, and pin. Stitch the front and back sections together. Start from the pig's shoulder and work round, sewing the arm, both legs, and then the other arm. Use whipstitch and matching sewing threads, changing thread colors as needed and removing the pins as you sew each section.

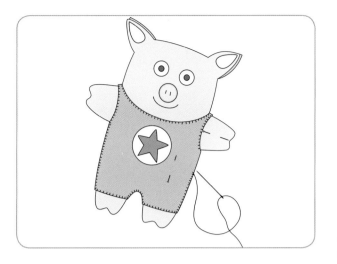

11 Fill the pig's arms, legs and body with stuffing. Add small pieces of stuffing at a time, filling the shapes firmly.

12 Pin the stitch guide to the pig's head, and use it to mark the stitching lines on the pig's ears with the air erasable fabric marker. Remove the guide.

13 Begin sewing around the head, using pins as needed to hold the front and back together. Use whipstitch and matching pink sewing thread, following the stitching line when sewing across the bottom of the ears. Stitch most of the way around the head, leaving a gap for stuffing.

14 Stuff the head firmly, then close up the remaining gap with more whipstitches.

15 Finish the pig by stitching the front and back of each ear together with whipstitch and matching thread.

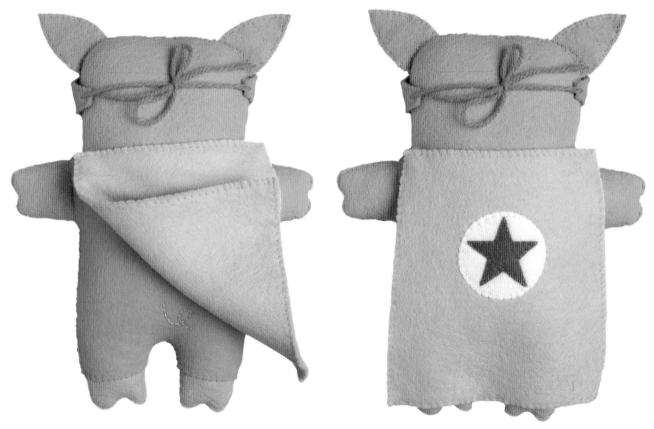

Make the Cape

1 Use the template provided to cut out the cape pieces from felt.

2 Sew the second circle and star shapes (cut out earlier) to one of the cape pieces, as pictured, using whipstitch and matching sewing threads.

3 Cut two lengths of yarn, each measuring approximately 10 inches (25.4 cm). Thread a large, sharp needle with one of the yarn pieces, and tie a large knot in the end. Use the needle to pass the yarn through the top corner of the undecorated cape piece. Repeat to add the second piece of yarn to the opposite corner.

4 Pin the two cape pieces together, sandwiching the yarn knots between them. Sew the edges of the cape together with whipstitch and matching sewing thread, removing the pins when they are no longer needed.

Make the Mask

1 Use the template provided to cut out the mask pieces from felt.

2 Pin the two mask pieces together and sew around the eye holes with whipstitch and matching sewing thread. Then remove the pins.

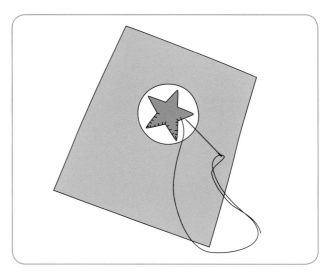

3 Cut two lengths of yarn, each measuring approximately 10 inches (25.4 cm). Thread a large, sharp needle with one of the yarn pieces, and tie a large knot in the end. Use the needle to pass the yarn through one side of the mask. Repeat to add the second piece of yarn to the other side.

4 Sew around the outside of the mask with more whipstitches and matching sewing thread.

> **TIP**
> **When the cape and mask are tied in place on the pig, trim the yarn as needed.**

SYLVIA THE BAKER SQUIRREL

DESIGNER: MOLLIE JOHANSON

Sylvia is just nutty about baking sweet treats! Actually, she's a little nutty all around. When she's working in the kitchen, Sylvia can be a bit absentminded, forgetting ingredients or adding extras. But that doesn't stop her from baking! In fact, her merry mix-ups have helped her create all kinds of fun new recipes that her forest friends simply love!

MATERIALS

Templates (page 102–105)

Light gray fleece, ⅓ yard (30.5 cm)

Dark gray fleece, ⅓ yard (30.5 cm)

Dark gray felt scrap

Pink felt for the hat, 6 x 9 inches
    (15.2 x 22.9 cm)

Pink felt for the cupcake frosting,
    3 x 3 inches (7.6 x 7.6 cm)

White felt for the apron, 2½ x 4½ inches
    (6.4 x 11.4 cm)

Brown felt for the cupcake, 3 x 3 inches
    (7.6 x 7.6 cm)

Tan and brown felt scraps

Threads to match the felt

Embroidery floss in black, pink, brown,
    and colors as desired for the cupcake
    sprinkles

Two 12 mm safety eyes

Stuffing

Fabric glue

1½-inch (3.8 cm) strip of hook-and-loop
    fastener

28 inches (71.1 cm) of ribbon or bias tape

3-inch (7.6 cm) piece of wide elastic
    (fold-over elastic works well)

TOOLS

Fabric scissors

Erasable marking pen

Hand-sewing needle

Embroidery needle

Straight pins

Sewing machine

NOTE
All seam allowances are
¼ inch (6 mm).

INSTRUCTIONS
Make the Squirrel

1 Cut two body pieces from light gray fleece and transfer the markings for the face onto one piece. Cut two tail pieces and four ear pieces from dark gray fleece. Cut eight arm/leg pieces from light gray fleece. Cut one nose piece from dark gray felt. Be sure to follow the stretch markings on the fleece pieces (see page xi).

2 On the front body piece, cut two tiny holes where the eyes will go and install the safety eyes. (If you will be giving this to a young child, embroider or appliqué the eyes instead.) Appliqué the felt nose in place with whipstitch (page x) and embroider the mouth with black floss using backstitch (page viii).

3 Pin two arm/leg pieces with right sides together and sew around the curved edge, leaving the straight edge open for turning. Repeat with all sets of arms and legs. Do the same with the ear pieces.

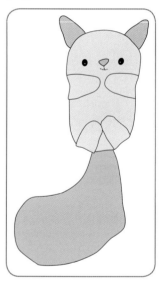

4 Pin the tail pieces with right sides together and sew around the shape, leaving the two marked areas open. Clip the curves (see page xi), then turn the tail right side out.

5 Place the back body piece right side up, then lay the ears, arms, legs, and tail on top, with raw edges aligning with the edge of the body piece and the finished sides facing in. Baste the pieces in place.

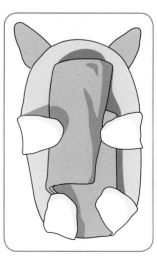

6 Fold the tail in, then pin the front body piece to the back with right sides together. Sew around the sides, leaving an opening for turning. Clip the curves, then turn the body right side out.

7 Stuff the tail and the body, and sew the openings closed with ladder stitch using matching thread (page ix).

8 Fold the tail up to the back of the body and use fabric glue to attach the hook-and-loop fastener so the tail can be up or down behind the body.

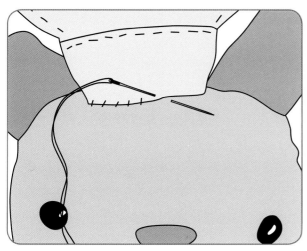

Make the Hat

Cut two hat top pieces and one 1 x 5½-inch (2.5 x 14 cm) rectangle from pink felt. Stitch the top pieces together with running stitch (page ix), adding a bit of stuffing before closing it up. Stitch the rectangle into a loop with ¼-inch (6 mm) overlap. Insert the hat top into the loop and stitch across the top of the loop with running stitch through all of the layers. Set the hat on top of Sylvia's head and open the base of the hat. Stitch the hat to Sylvia's head with whipstitch and matching thread.

Make the Apron

Cut the acorn pieces from tan and brown felt. Embroider the face onto the bottom part of the acorn. Use fabric glue to attach the acorn pieces to the white rectangle of felt. Center the ribbon or bias tape across the apron front and stitch it in place along the top of the felt with two rows of running stitch.

Make the Cupcake

Cut two cupcake top pieces from pink felt and two cupcake bottom pieces from brown felt. Embroider sprinkles on one of the cupcake tops. Stitch the cupcake top pieces to the bottom pieces with running stitch so the top overlaps the bottom. Sew the elastic to the back cupcake piece on the right side. Leave some slack so there's room for Sylvia's hand to slip through. Stitch the two cupcake pieces together with running stitch.

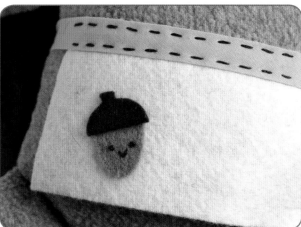

PROJECT TEMPLATES

ADVENTURER BEAR

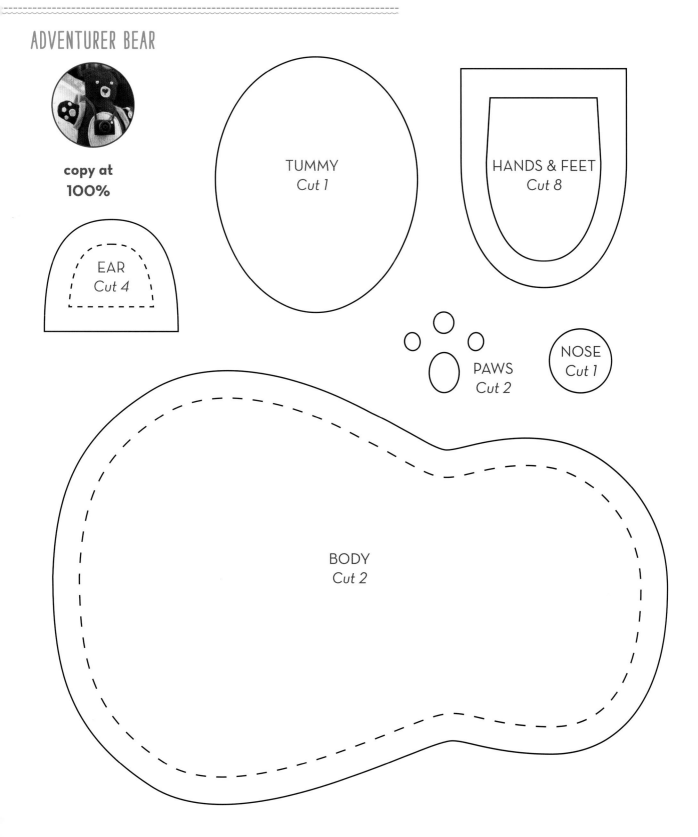

copy at
100%

EAR
Cut 4

TUMMY
Cut 1

HANDS & FEET
Cut 8

PAWS
Cut 2

NOSE
Cut 1

BODY
Cut 2

MAP
Cut 1

**copy at
100%**

BACKPACK STRAPS   *Cut 2*

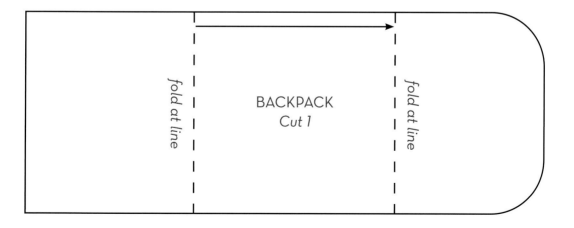

fold at line

BACKPACK
Cut 1

fold at line

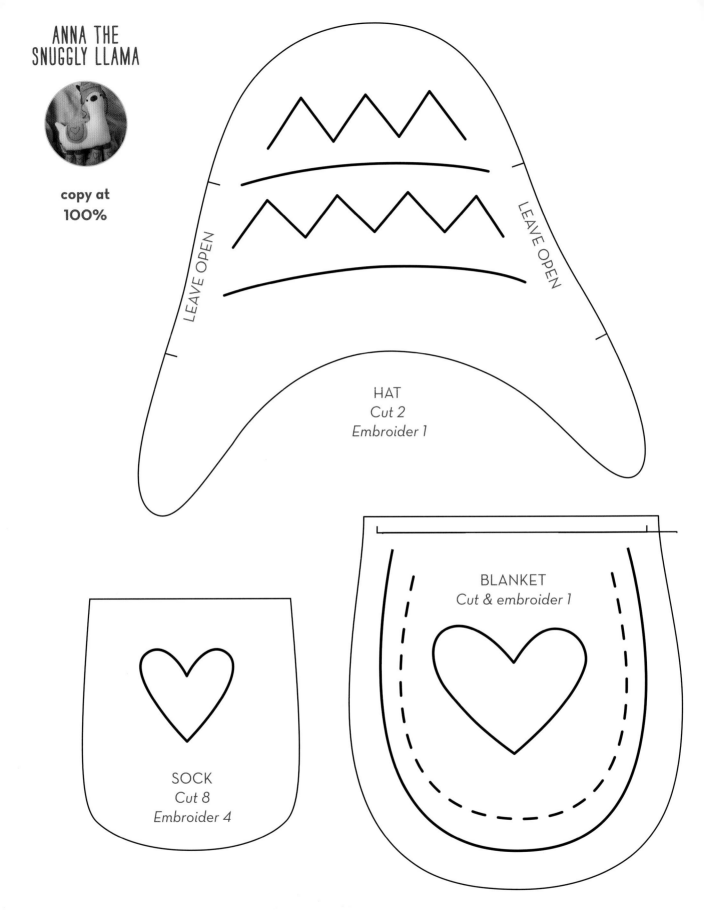

ANNA THE
SNUGGLY LLAMA

copy at
100%

LEAVE OPEN

LEAVE OPEN

HAT
Cut 2
Embroider 1

BLANKET
Cut & embroider 1

SOCK
Cut 8
Embroider 4

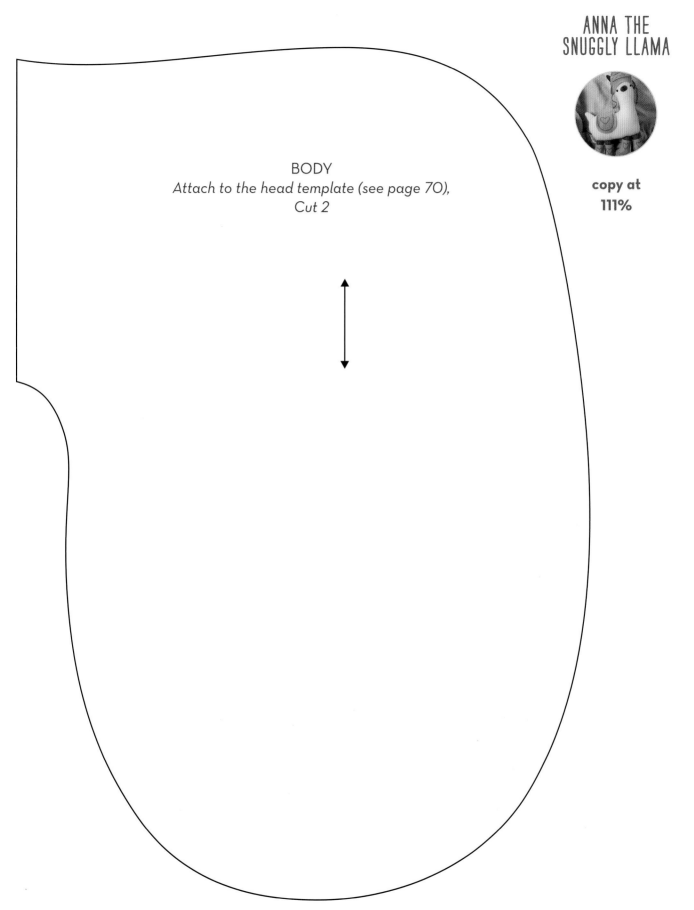

copy at
111%

BODY
Attach to the head template (see page 70),
Cut 2

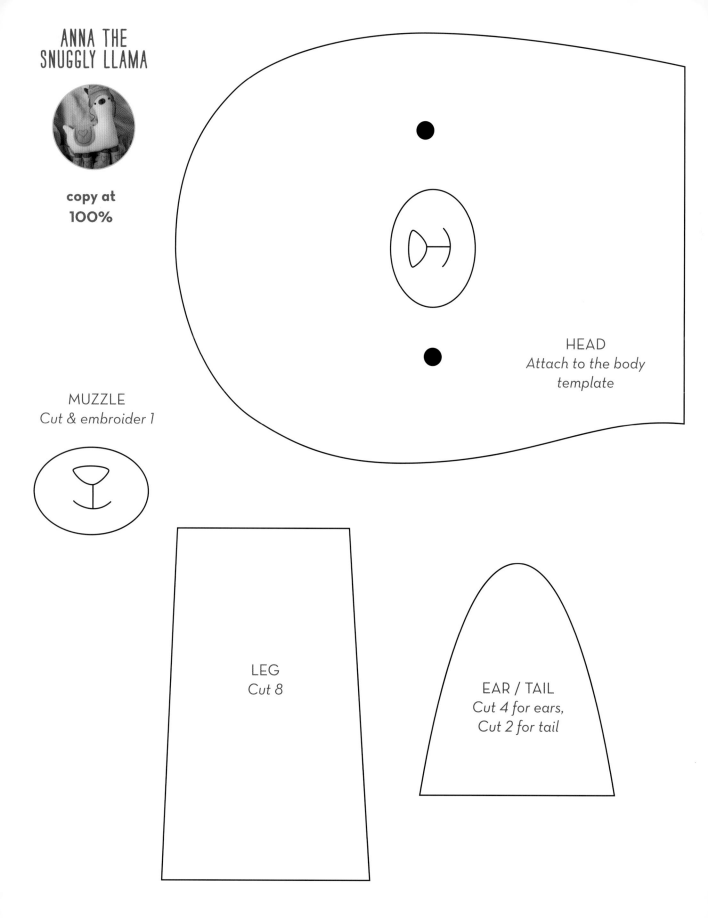

ANNA THE
SNUGGLY LLAMA

copy at
100%

HEAD
*Attach to the body
template*

MUZZLE
Cut & embroider 1

LEG
Cut 8

EAR / TAIL
*Cut 4 for ears,
Cut 2 for tail*

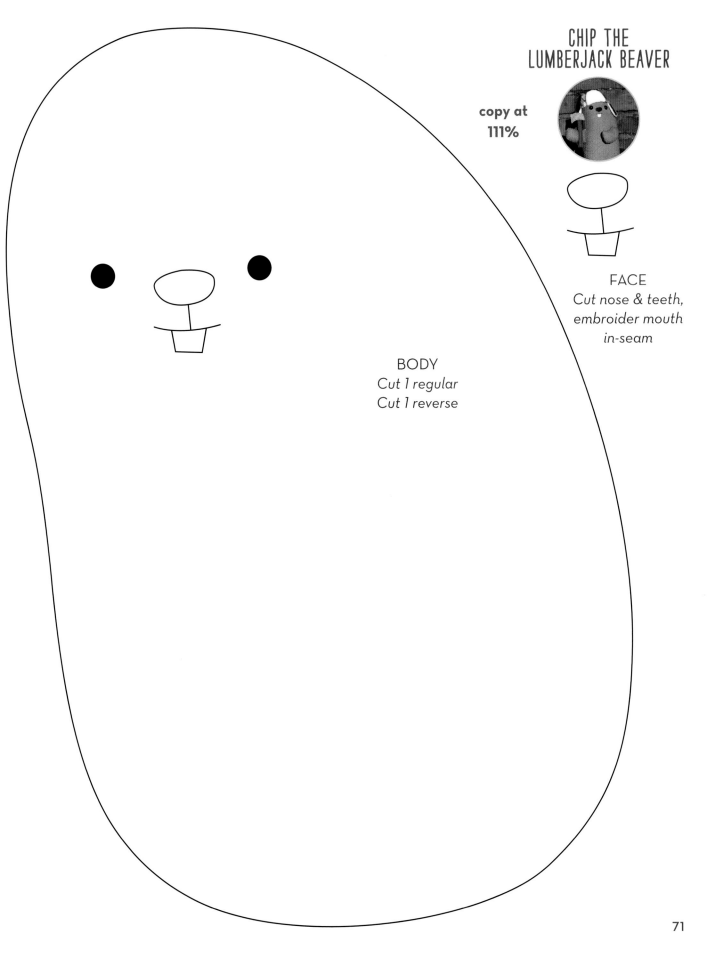

CHIP THE
LUMBERJACK BEAVER

copy at
111%

FACE
*Cut nose & teeth,
embroider mouth
in-seam*

BODY
*Cut 1 regular
Cut 1 reverse*

71

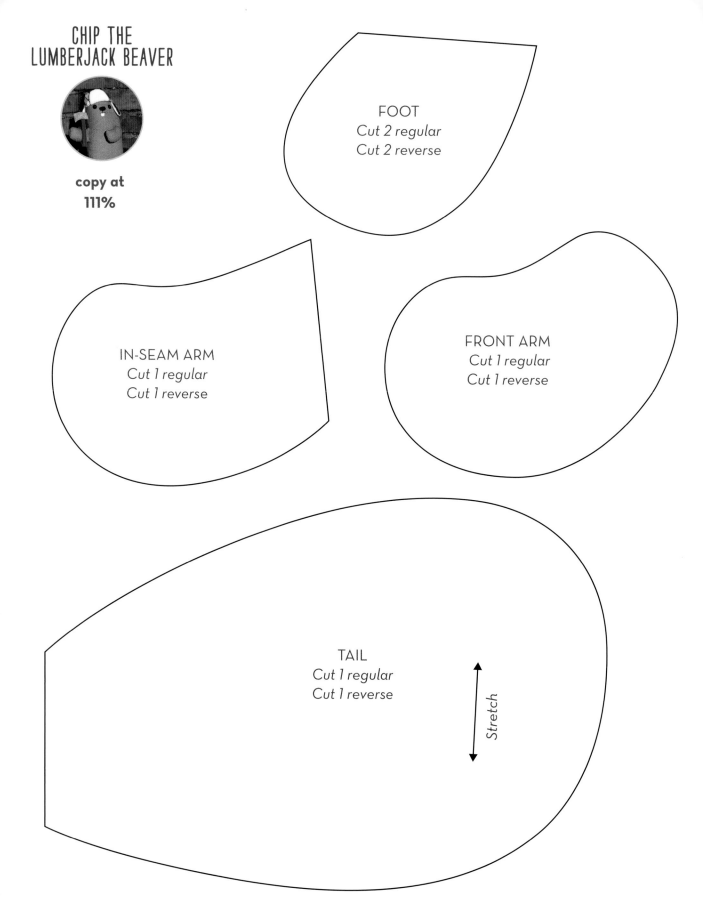

CHIP THE LUMBERJACK BEAVER

copy at
111%

FOOT
Cut 2 regular
Cut 2 reverse

IN-SEAM ARM
Cut 1 regular
Cut 1 reverse

FRONT ARM
Cut 1 regular
Cut 1 reverse

TAIL
Cut 1 regular
Cut 1 reverse

Stretch

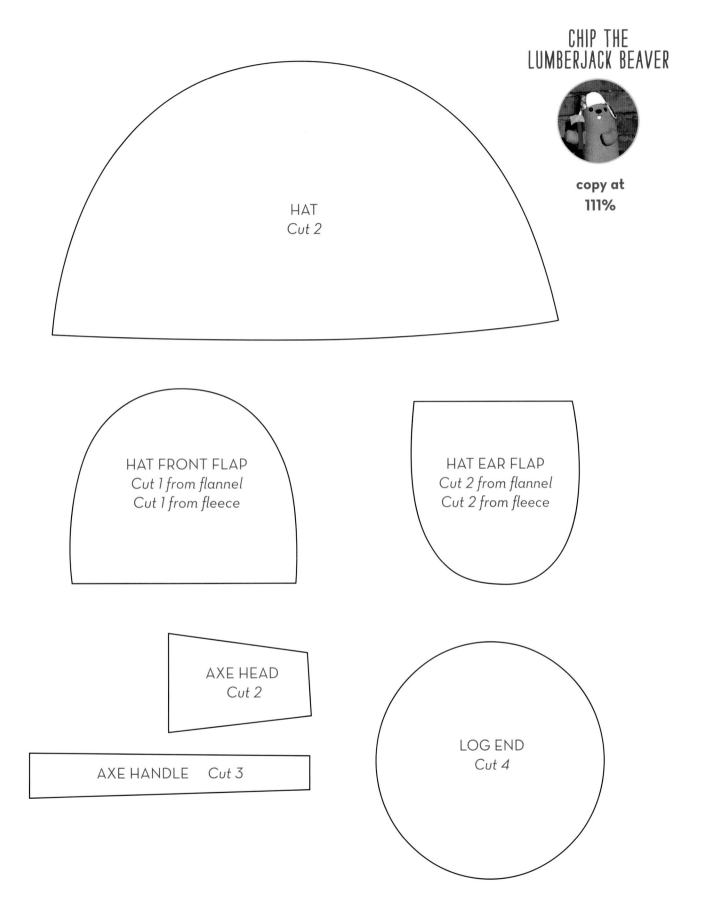

CHIP THE
LUMBERJACK BEAVER

copy at
111%

HAT
Cut 2

HAT FRONT FLAP
Cut 1 from flannel
Cut 1 from fleece

HAT EAR FLAP
Cut 2 from flannel
Cut 2 from fleece

AXE HEAD
Cut 2

AXE HANDLE   Cut 3

LOG END
Cut 4

CRAFTY BUNNY

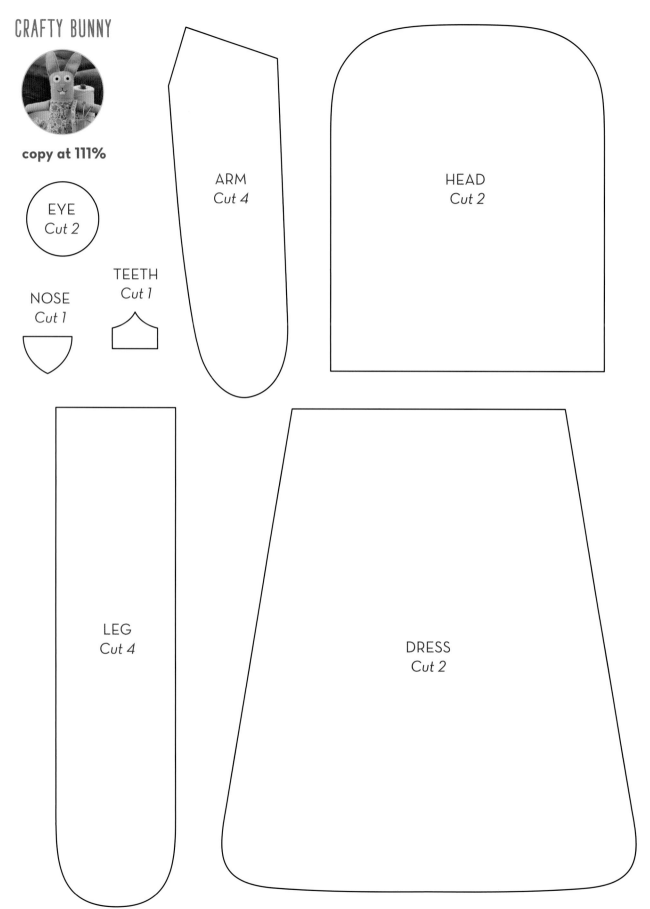

copy at 111%

EYE
Cut 2

NOSE
Cut 1

TEETH
Cut 1

ARM
Cut 4

HEAD
Cut 2

LEG
Cut 4

DRESS
Cut 2

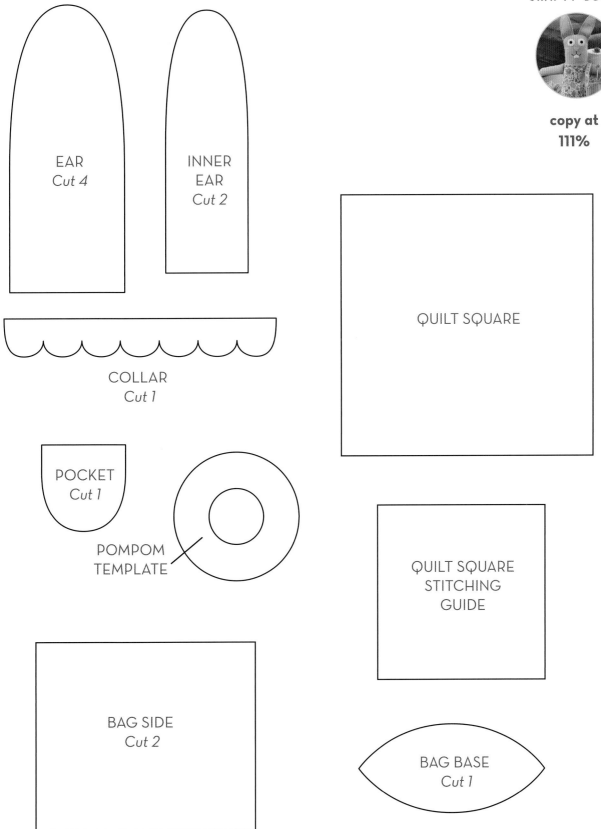

**copy at
111%**

EAR
Cut 4

INNER
EAR
Cut 2

COLLAR
Cut 1

QUILT SQUARE

POCKET
Cut 1

POMPOM
TEMPLATE

QUILT SQUARE
STITCHING
GUIDE

BAG SIDE
Cut 2

BAG BASE
Cut 1

FAIRY MOUSE

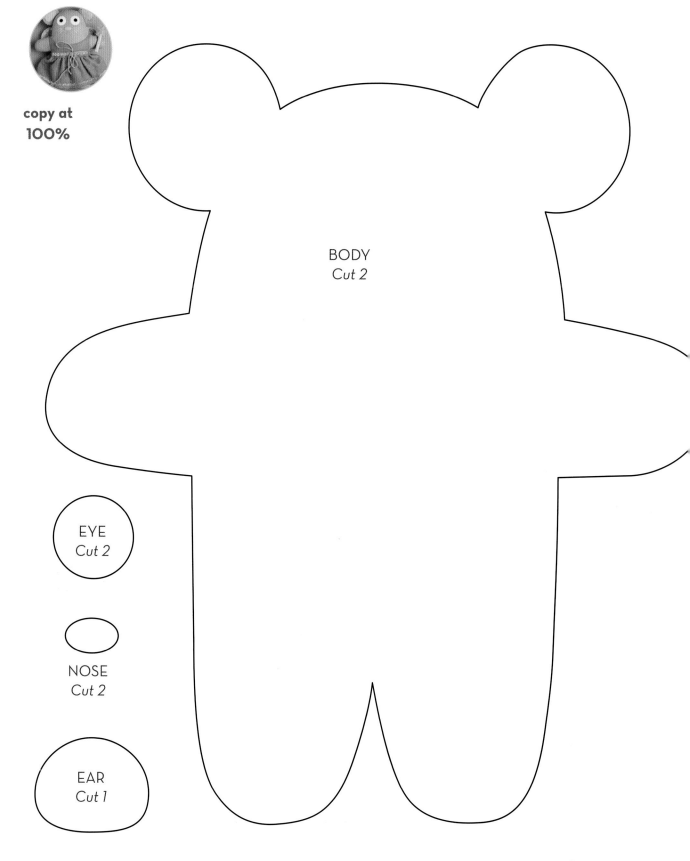

copy at
100%

BODY
Cut 2

EYE
Cut 2

NOSE
Cut 2

EAR
Cut 1

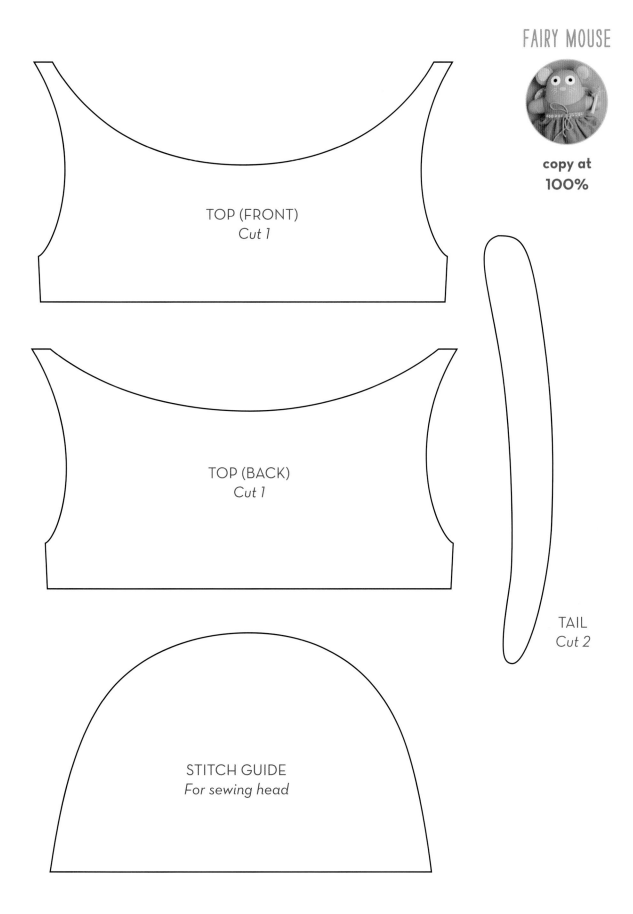

TOP (FRONT)
Cut 1

TOP (BACK)
Cut 1

TAIL
Cut 2

STITCH GUIDE
For sewing head

FAIRY MOUSE

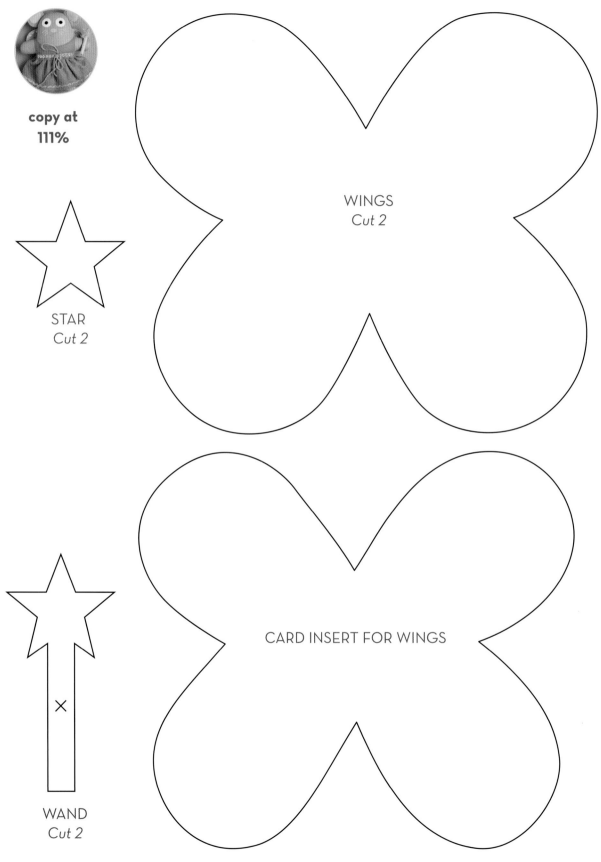

copy at 111%

WINGS
Cut 2

STAR
Cut 2

CARD INSERT FOR WINGS

WAND
Cut 2

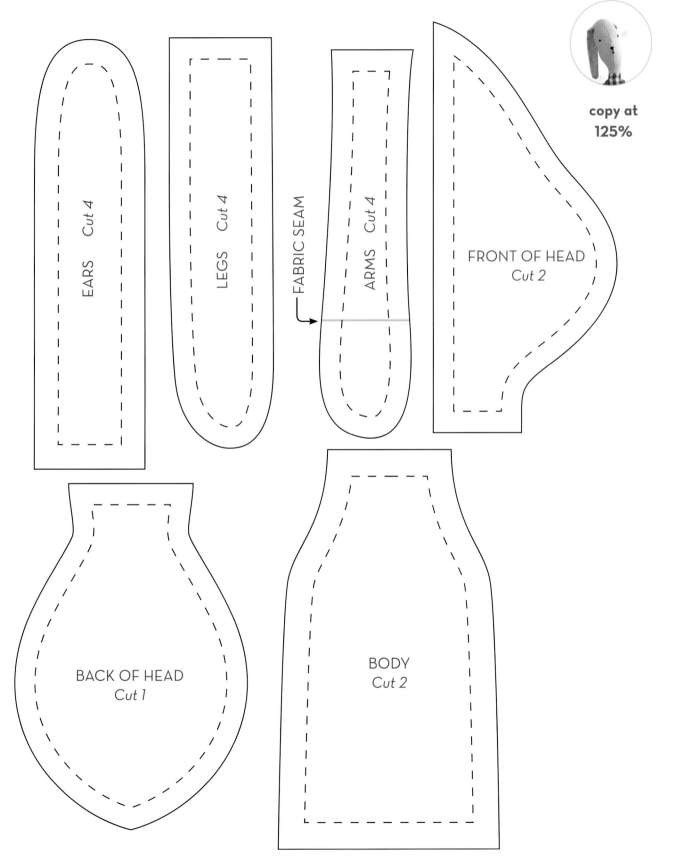

copy at
125%

EARS   Cut 4

LEGS   Cut 4

FABRIC SEAM

ARMS   Cut 4

FRONT OF HEAD
Cut 2

BACK OF HEAD
Cut 1

BODY
Cut 2

FARMER HARE

copy at 100%

OVERALL STRAP Cut 2

OVERALL TOP
Cut 2

FOLD

OVERALL PANT LEGS
Cut 2 on fold

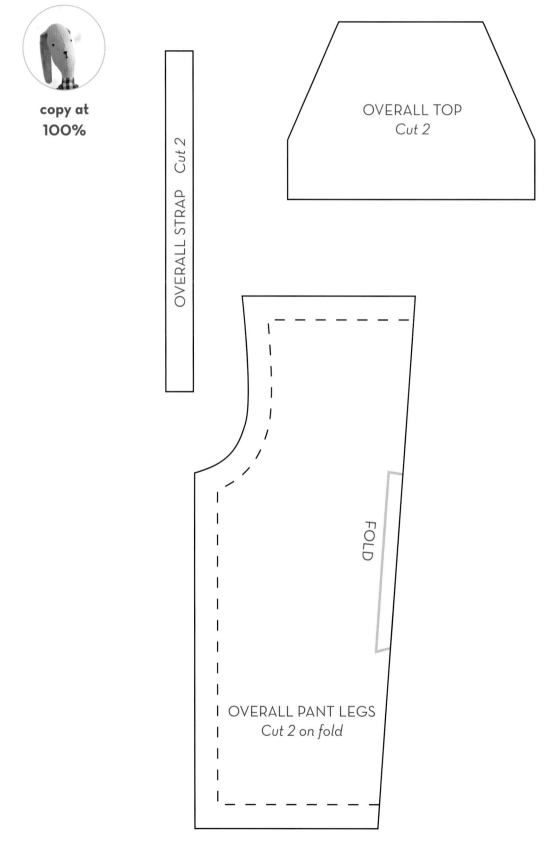

BASKET SIDE
Cut 1

BASKET HANDLE   Cut 1

BASKET BOTTOM
Cut 1

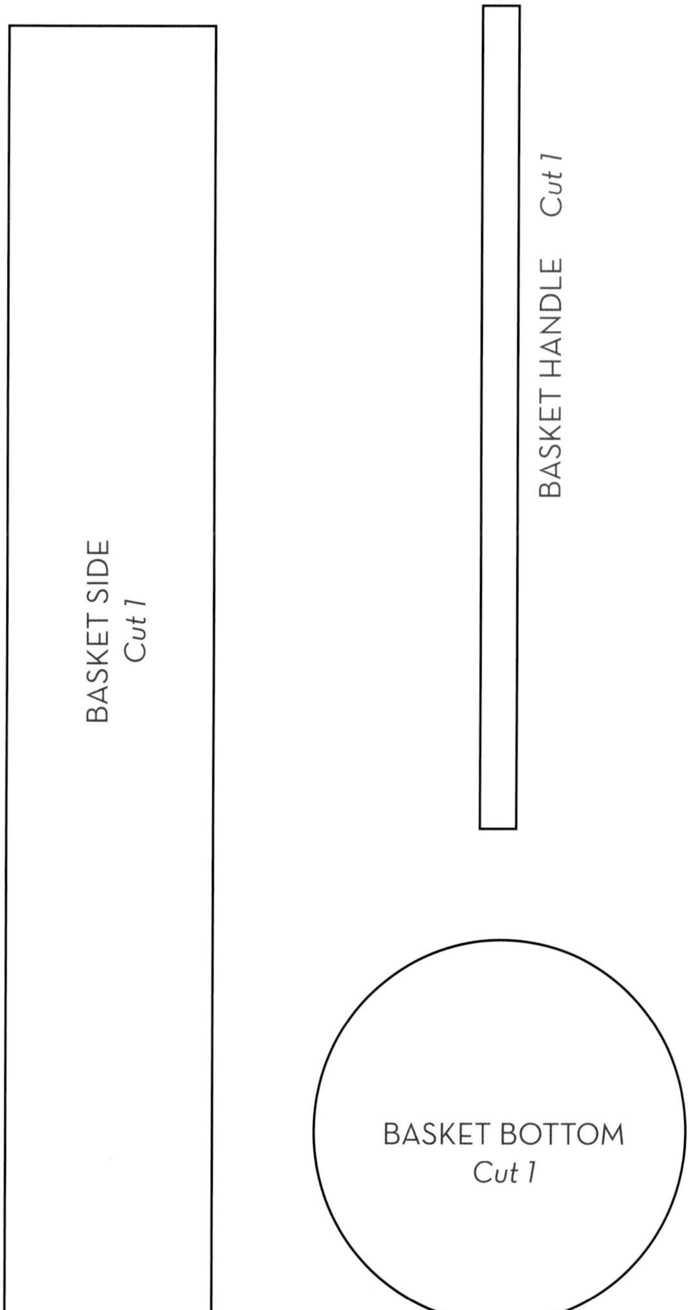

FESTIVAL PANDA

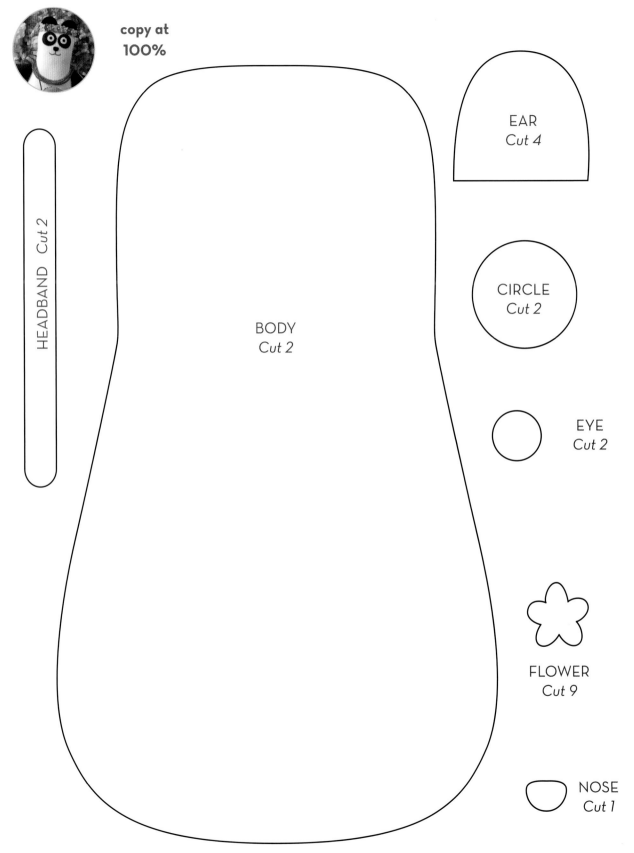

copy at
100%

EAR
Cut 4

HEADBAND *Cut 2*

CIRCLE
Cut 2

BODY
Cut 2

EYE
Cut 2

FLOWER
Cut 9

NOSE
Cut 1

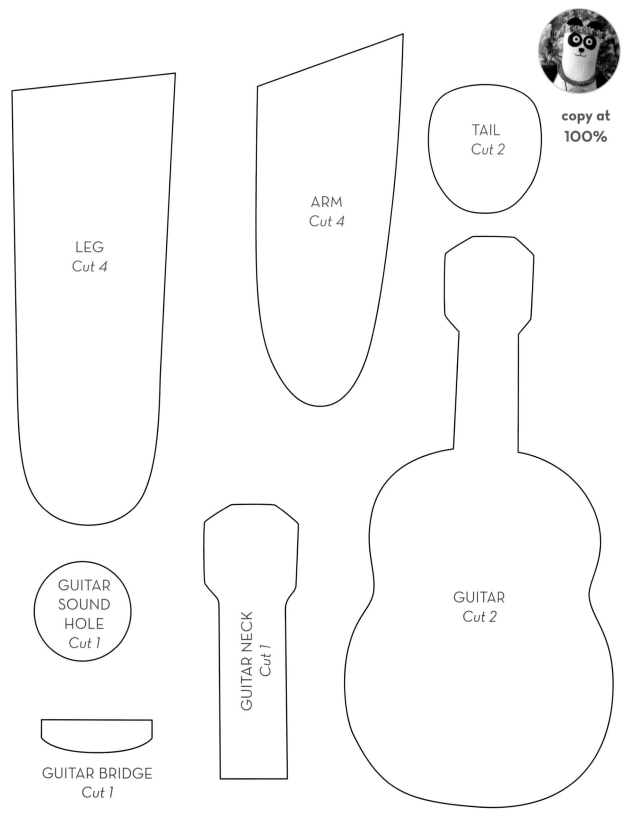

copy at
100%

LEG
Cut 4

ARM
Cut 4

TAIL
Cut 2

GUITAR
SOUND
HOLE
Cut 1

GUITAR NECK
Cut 1

GUITAR
Cut 2

GUITAR BRIDGE
Cut 1

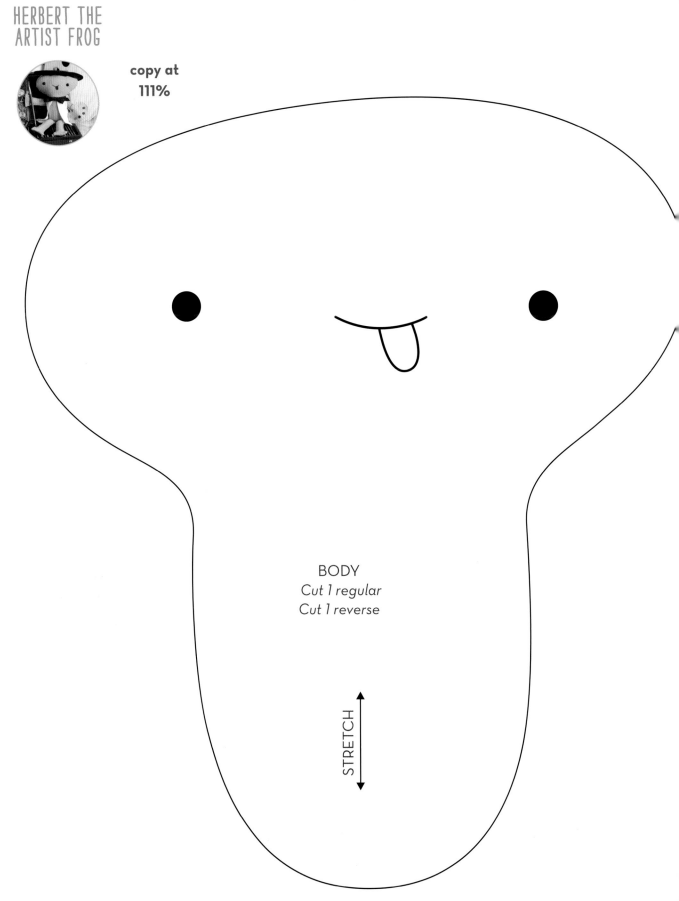

**copy at
111%**

BODY
Cut 1 regular
Cut 1 reverse

STRETCH

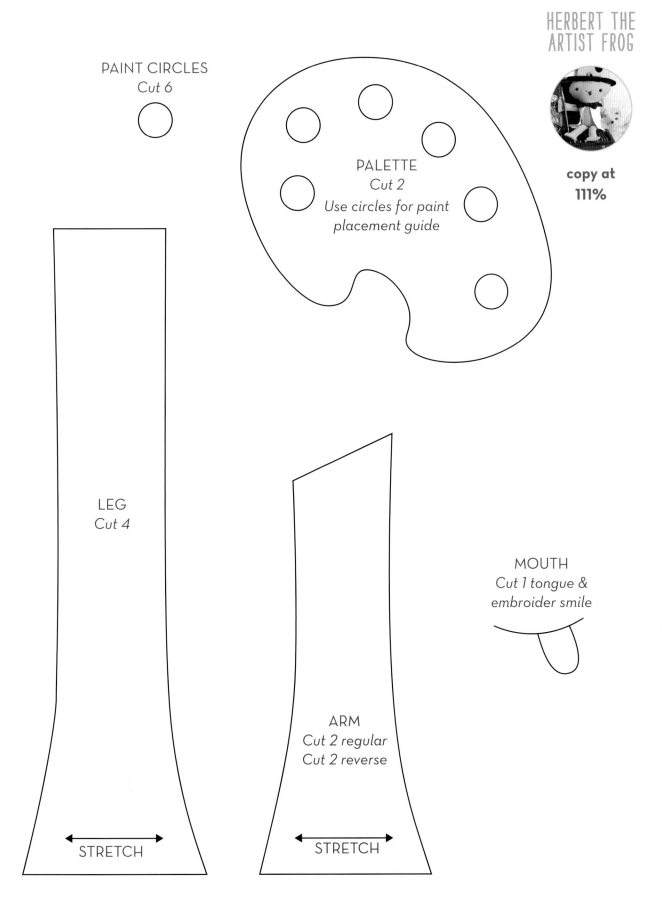

copy at
111%

PAINT CIRCLES
Cut 6

PALETTE
Cut 2
Use circles for paint
placement guide

LEG
Cut 4

MOUTH
Cut 1 tongue &
embroider smile

ARM
Cut 2 regular
Cut 2 reverse

STRETCH

STRETCH

copy at
100%

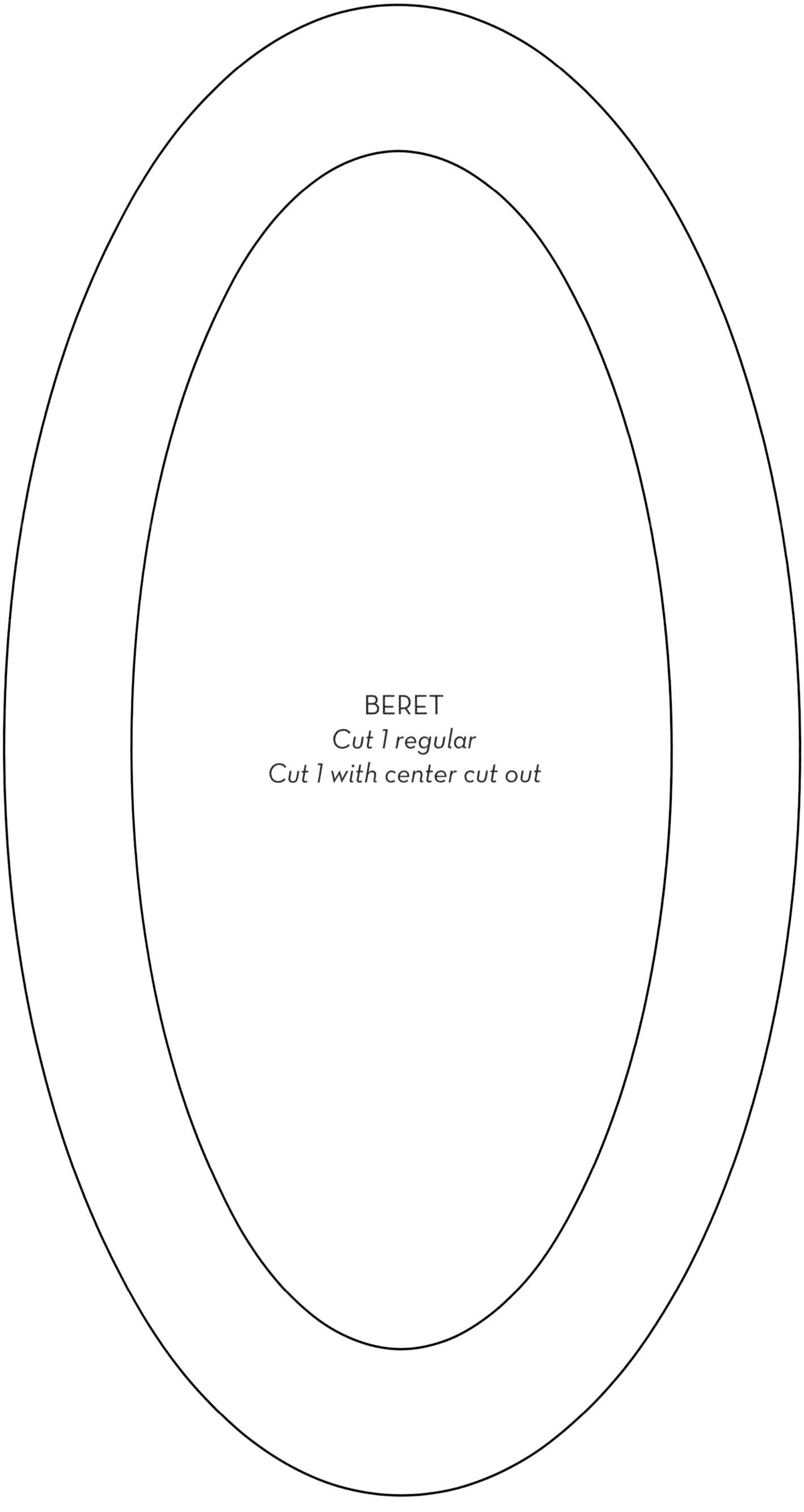

BERET
Cut 1 regular
Cut 1 with center cut out

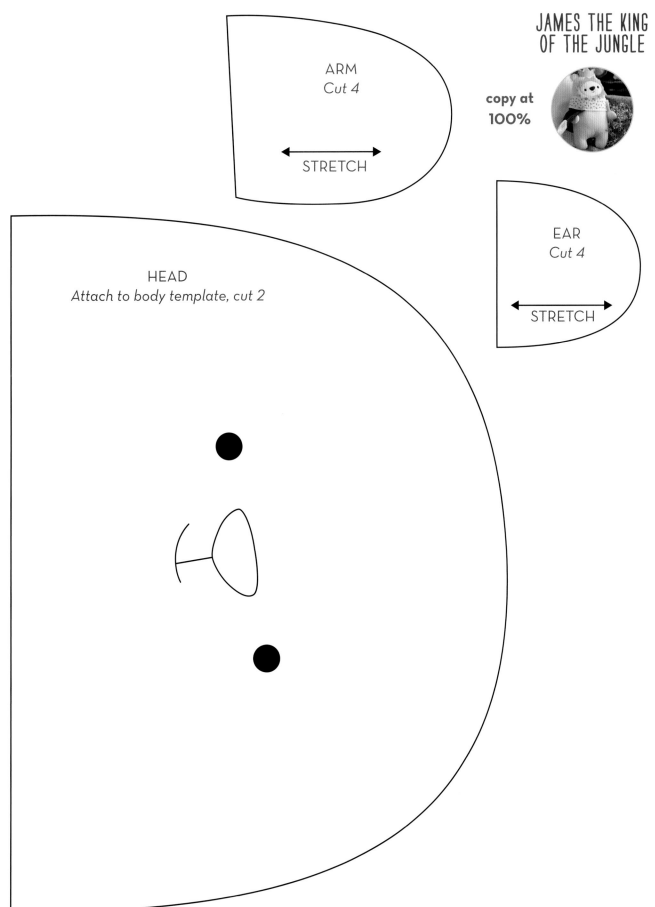

ARM
Cut 4

STRETCH

copy at
100%

EAR
Cut 4

STRETCH

HEAD
Attach to body template, cut 2

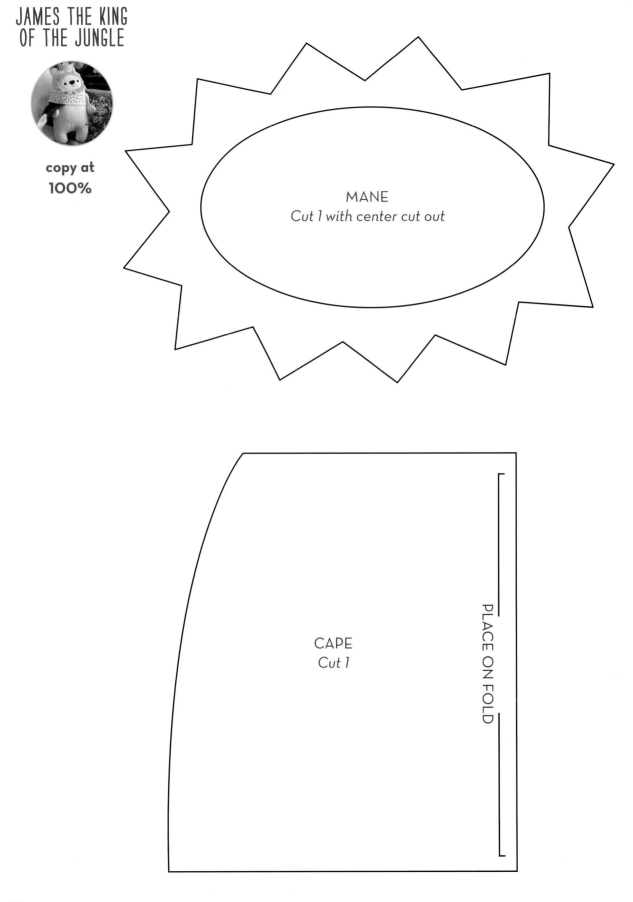

copy at
100%

MANE
Cut 1 with center cut out

CAPE
Cut 1

PLACE ON FOLD

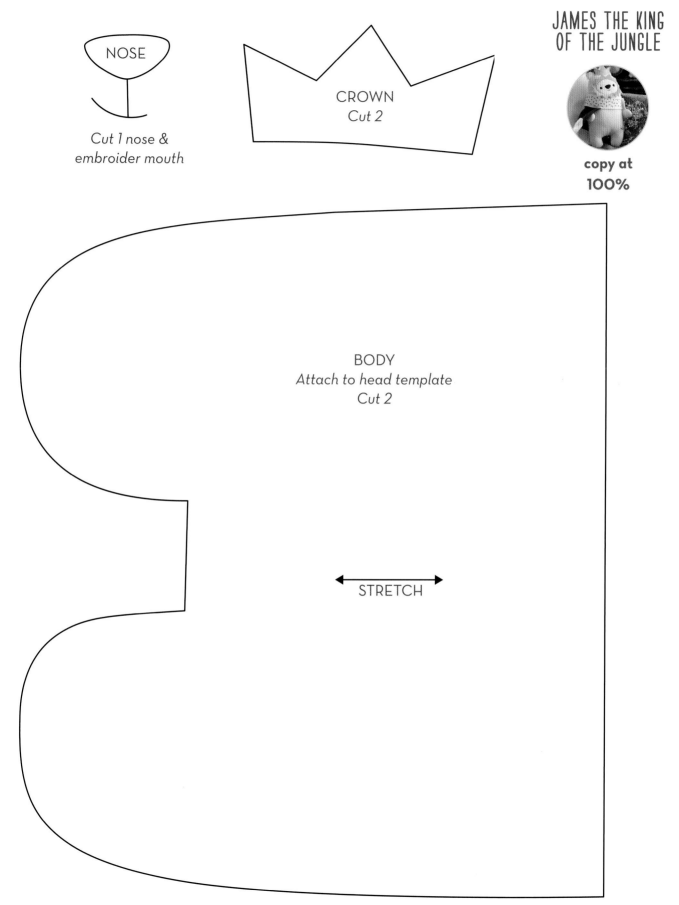

NOSE

Cut 1 nose &
embroider mouth

CROWN
Cut 2

JAMES THE KING
OF THE JUNGLE

**copy at
100%**

BODY
Attach to head template
Cut 2

STRETCH

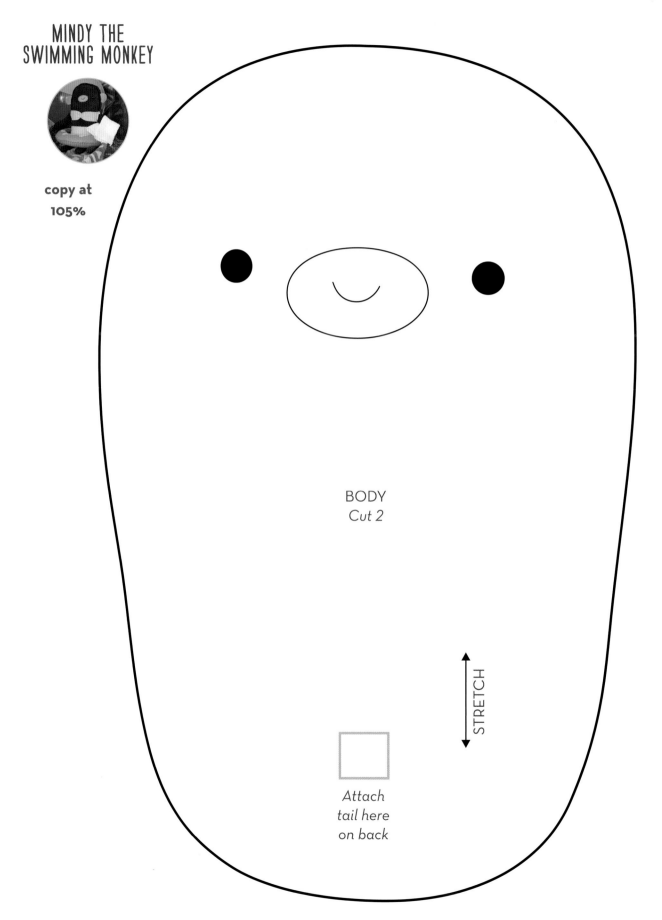

MINDY THE
SWIMMING MONKEY

copy at
105%

BODY
Cut 2

STRETCH

Attach
tail here
on back

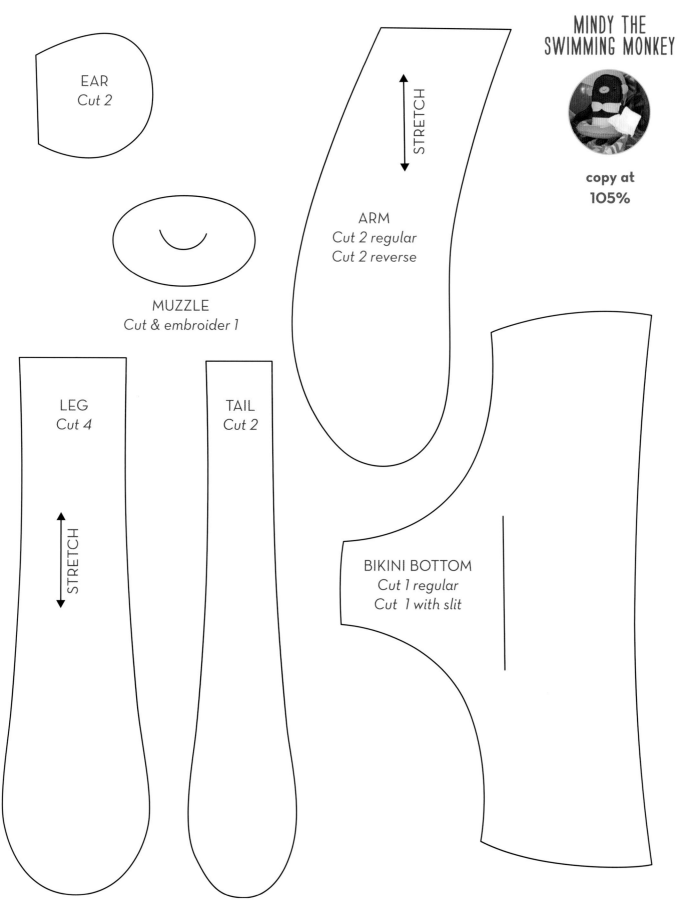

EAR
Cut 2

MUZZLE
Cut & embroider 1

STRETCH

ARM
Cut 2 regular
Cut 2 reverse

LEG
Cut 4

STRETCH

TAIL
Cut 2

BIKINI BOTTOM
Cut 1 regular
Cut 1 with slit

MINDY THE
SWIMMING MONKEY

copy at 105%

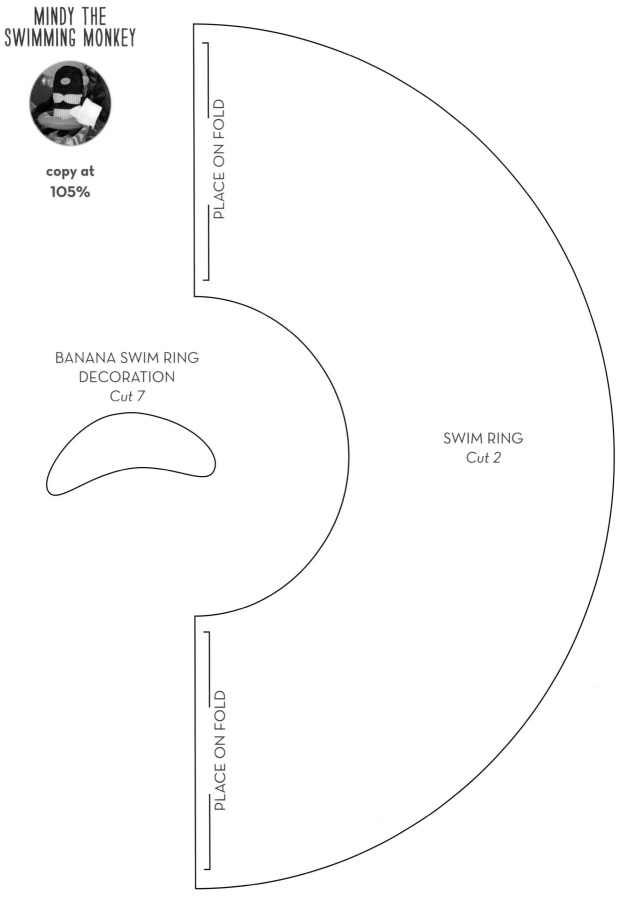

MINDY THE SWIMMING MONKEY

**copy at
105%**

BANANA SWIM RING
DECORATION
Cut 7

PLACE ON FOLD

SWIM RING
Cut 2

PLACE ON FOLD

copy at 100%

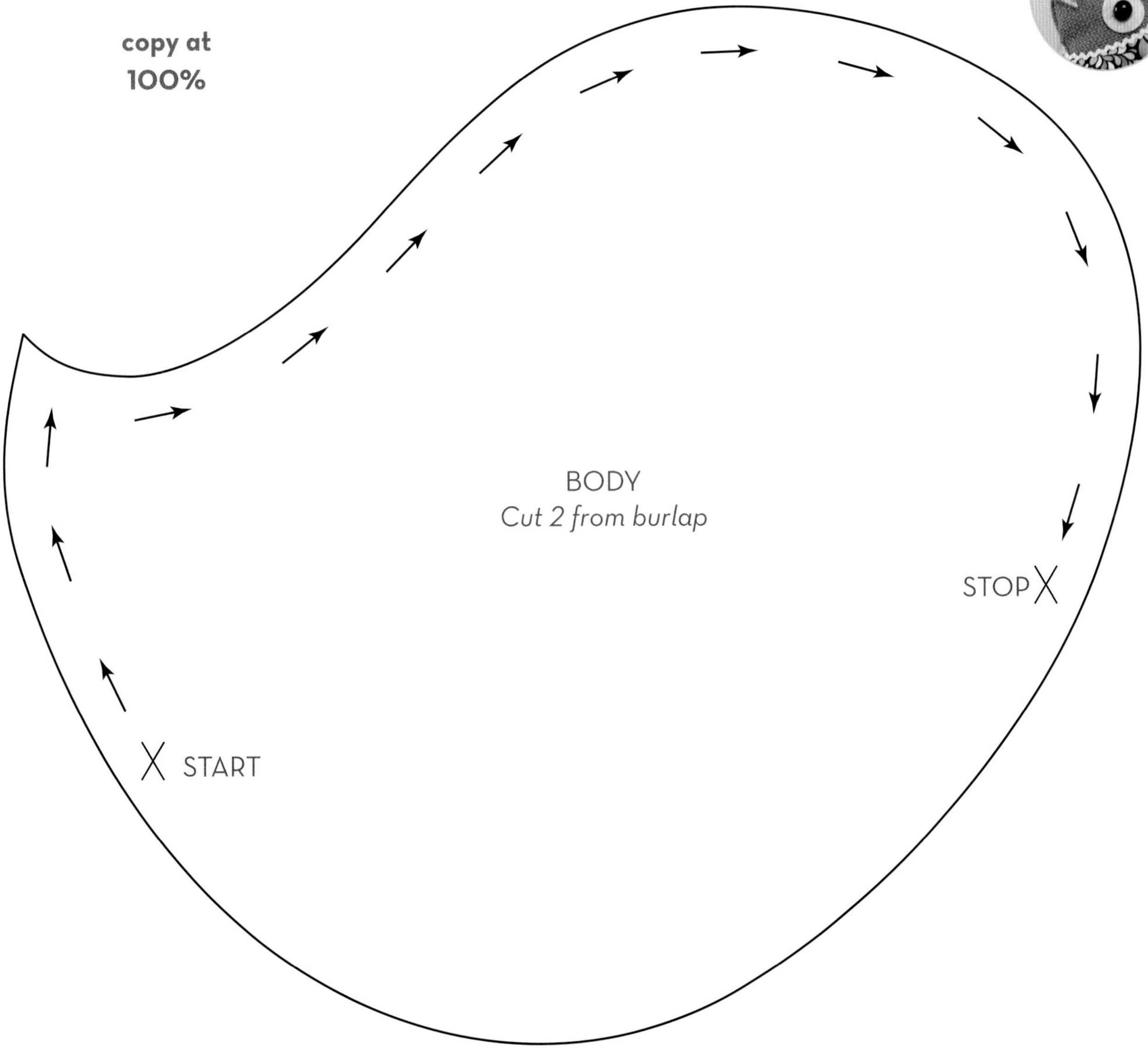

BODY
Cut 2 from burlap

✗ START

STOP ✗

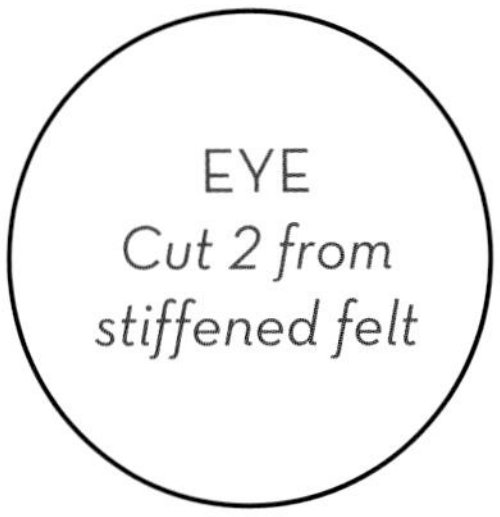

EYE
Cut 2 from stiffened felt

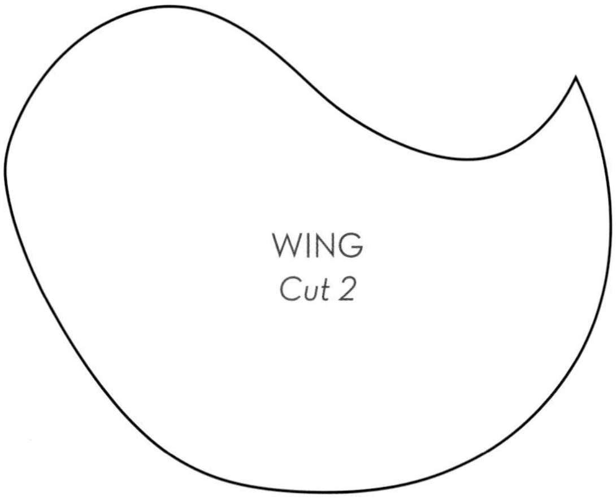

WING
Cut 2

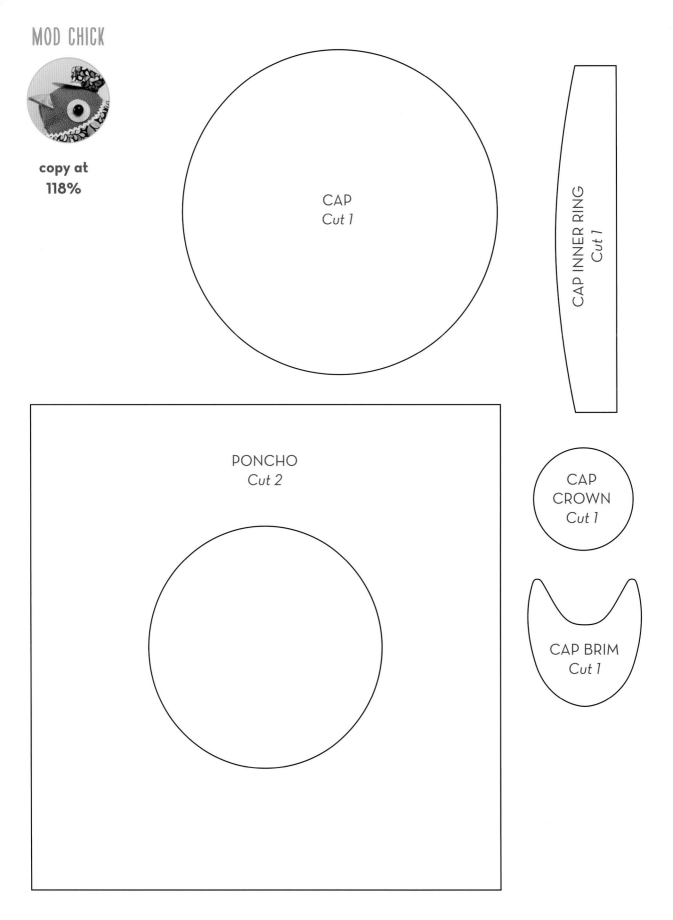

MOD CHICK

copy at 118%

CAP
Cut 1

CAP INNER RING
Cut 1

PONCHO
Cut 2

CAP CROWN
Cut 1

CAP BRIM
Cut 1

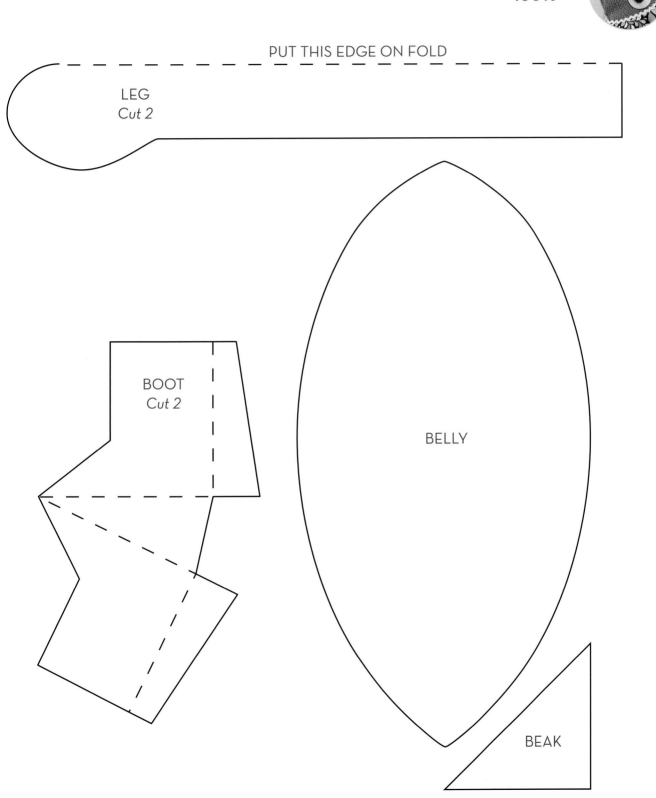

copy at
100%

PUT THIS EDGE ON FOLD

LEG
Cut 2

BOOT
Cut 2

BELLY

BEAK

OWL AND PUSSYCAT

copy at
118%

SHIRT BACK
Cut 2

SHIRT FRONT
Cut 1

Sew here

KITTY HEAD
Cut 2

BUTTON
Cut 1

KITTY BODY
Cut 2

OWL EYE
PIECE
Cut 1

OWL BELLY
Cut 1

OWL BODY
Cut 2

OWL WING
Cut 2

BOOK
MOON
Cut 1

BOOK COVER
Cut 1

CLOUD PILLOW
Cut 2

BOOK PAGE
Cut 1

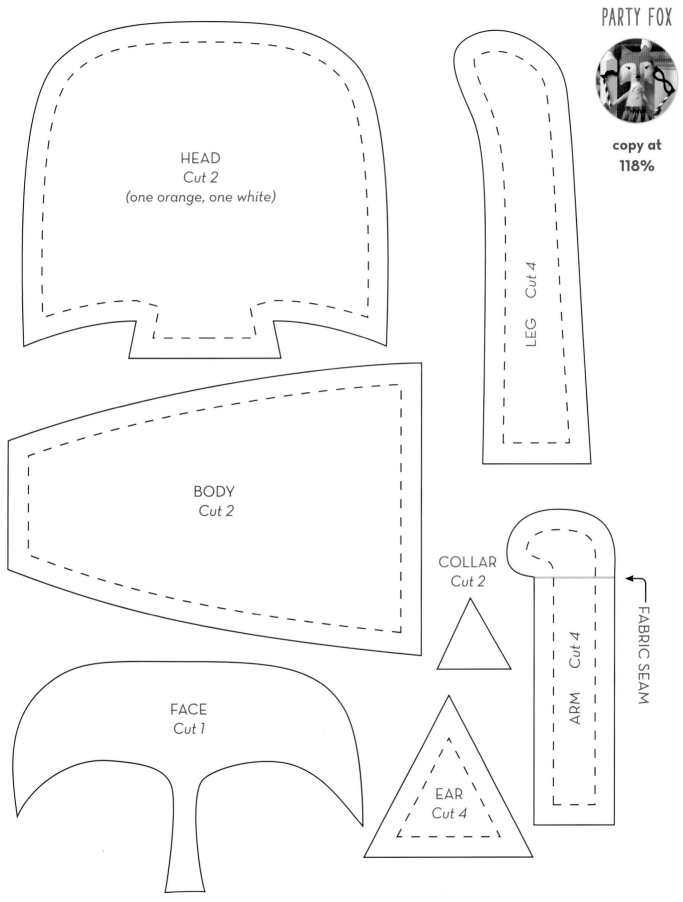

PARTY FOX

copy at 118%

HEAD
Cut 2
(one orange, one white)

LEG   *Cut 4*

BODY
Cut 2

COLLAR
Cut 2

FABRIC SEAM

ARM   *Cut 4*

FACE
Cut 1

EAR
Cut 4

**copy at
100%**

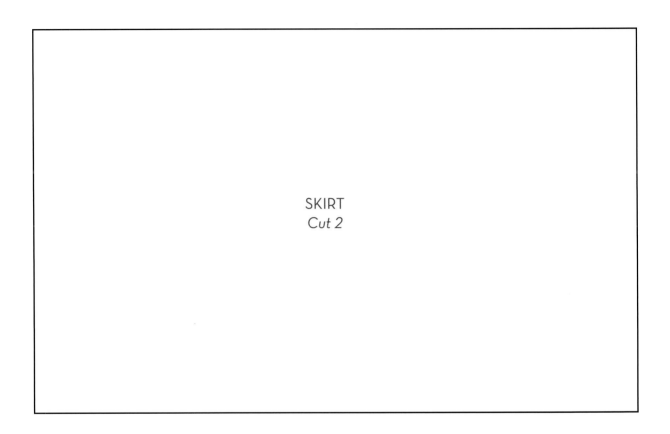

SKIRT
Cut 2

PHOTO PROPS

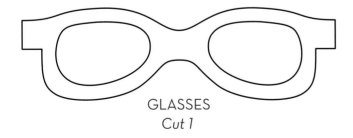

GLASSES
Cut 1

MOUSTACHE
Cut 1

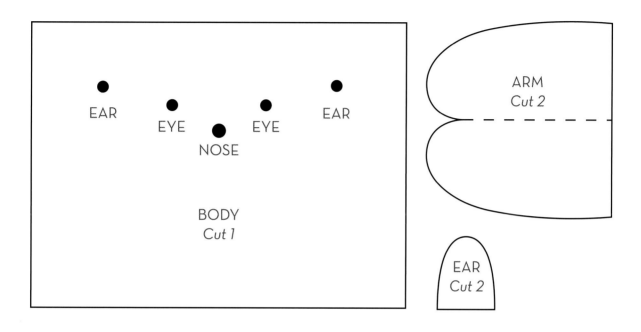

EAR

EYE

● NOSE

EYE

EAR

BODY
Cut 1

ARM
Cut 2

EAR
Cut 2

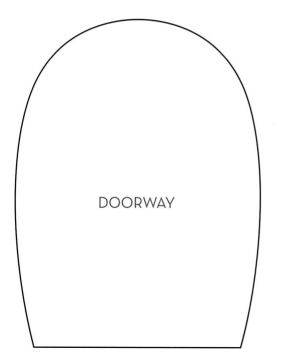

DOORWAY

SUPERHERO PIG

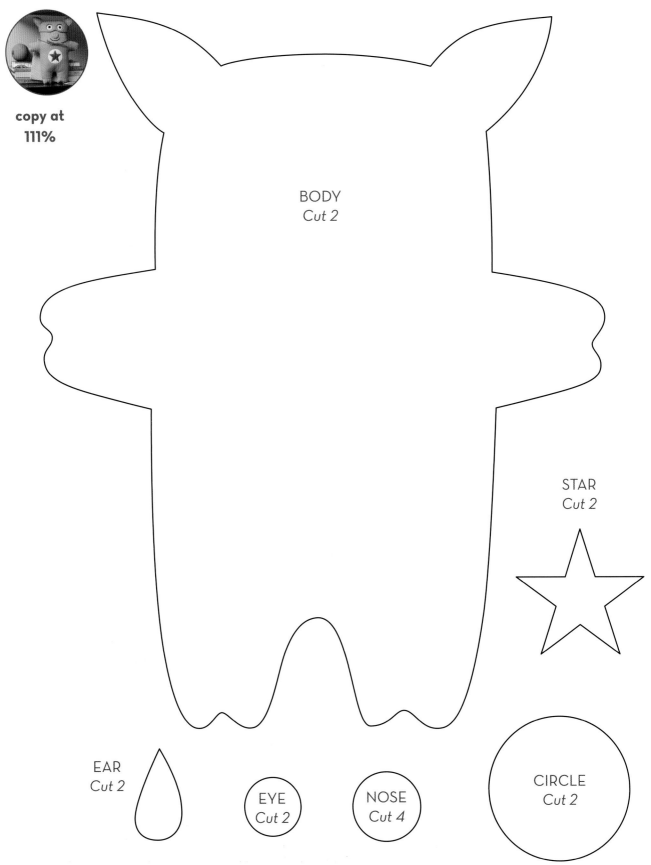

copy at
111%

BODY
Cut 2

STAR
Cut 2

EAR
Cut 2

EYE
Cut 2

NOSE
Cut 4

CIRCLE
Cut 2

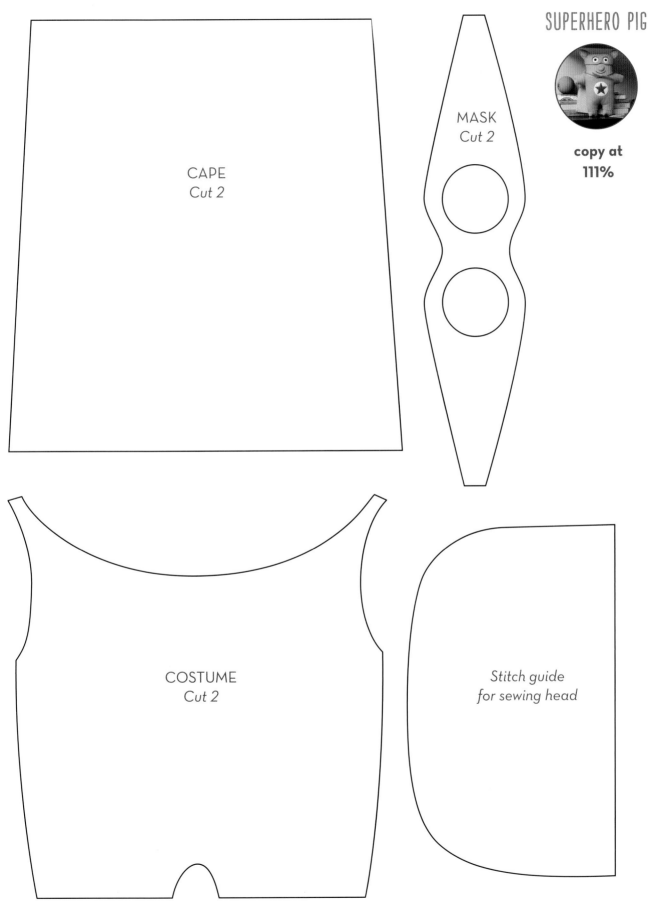

CAPE
Cut 2

MASK
Cut 2

**copy at
111%**

COSTUME
Cut 2

*Stitch guide
for sewing head*

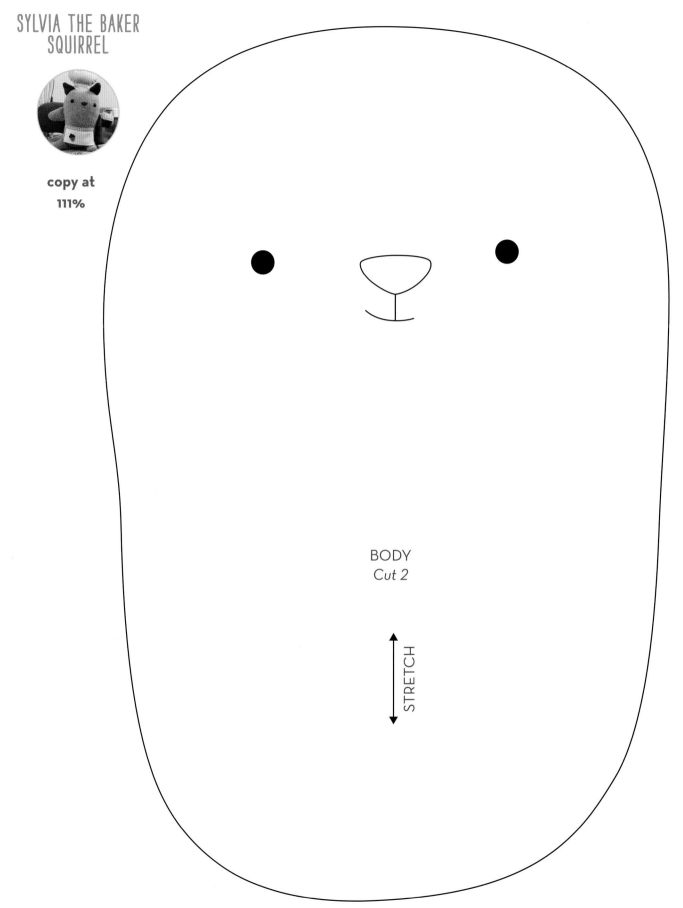

SYLVIA THE BAKER
SQUIRREL

copy at
111%

BODY
Cut 2

STRETCH

102

EAR
Cut 4

STRETCH

copy at
111%

HAT TOP
Cut 2

ARM / LEG
Cut 4

STRETCH

FACE
*Cut 1 nose &
embroider mouth*

CUPCAKE TOP
Cut 2

ACORN FOR APRON
*Cut 1 of each piece
& embroider face*

CUPCAKE
BOTTOM
Cut 2

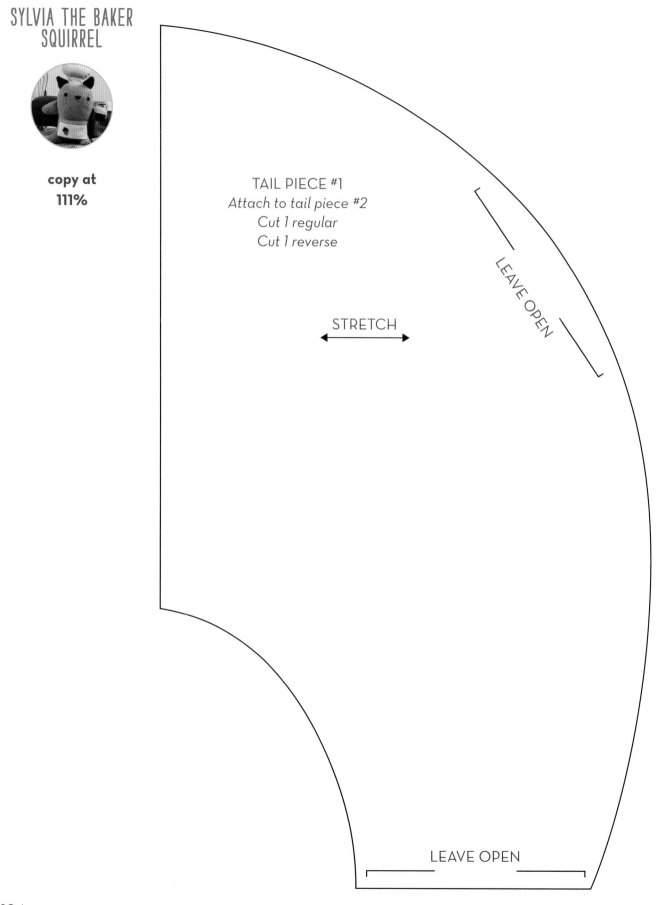

SYLVIA THE BAKER SQUIRREL

copy at 111%

TAIL PIECE #1
Attach to tail piece #2
Cut 1 regular
Cut 1 reverse

STRETCH

LEAVE OPEN

LEAVE OPEN

TAIL PIECE #2
Attach to tail piece #1

**copy at
100%**

ABOUT THE DESIGNERS

JESSICA FEDIW

As a military wife and devoted mother of two, Jessica has traveled throughout the East Coast and Gulf states, splitting her time and energy between raising a young family and channeling her creative passions. Early on, Jessica began sewing as a way to make one-of-a-kind outfits for her daughter. She took to blogging online and founded Happy Together (www.happytogetherbyjess.com) to capture her journey and share her experiences with others. Eventually, she expanded her creative interests to much more than just sewing. Jessica is influencing others around the world with her genuine message that love, family, and happiness are found when we share life together.

LAURA HOWARD

Laura is a designer/maker and crafts writer living near London, England. She loves to make stuff, especially if it involves her favorite material: felt! She regularly contributes projects to craft books and magazines and she's the author of two books about felt crafting: *Super-Cute Felt* and *Super-Cute Felt Animals*. Laura shares free tutorials and writes about her crafty adventures on her blog, Bugs and Fishes (www.bugsandfishes.blogspot.com) and sells her work at www.lupin.bigcartel.com.

MOLLIE JOHANSON

Mollie Johanson has loved cute things, creative messes, and cuddly critters for as long as she can remember. Her blog Wild Olive (www.wildolive.blogspot.com/) is known for embroidery patterns, simply-stitched projects, and playful printables, most often featuring charming creations with smiling faces. Her work has been published in *Mollie Makes*, *Australian Homespun*, and a variety of books, including several Lark Crafts titles. Mollie lives near Chicago and is happiest with a cup of coffee, some stitching, and her family close at hand.

SUZIE MILLIONS

Suzie Millions is an artist and compulsive crafter. Her book, *The Complete Book of Retro Crafts*, was published by Lark in 2008 and is well worth a look-see. Her studio is profiled in the 2010 book *Where Women Create: Book of Inspiration: In the Studio and Behind the Scenes with Extraordinary Women*, and her work has been featured on Martha Stewart's blog. See more at www.suziemillions.com and www.behance.net/suewille.

AIMEE RAY

Aimee Ray has been making things from paper, fabric, and clay for as long as she can remember. As a graphic designer in the greeting card and comic book industries, with several personal projects always in the works, she is almost never without something creative in hand, or in mind. Her diverse interests include digital printing and illustration, sewing, and embroidery. She is the author of many Lark titles, including *Doodle Stitching: The Motif Collection* and *Aimee Ray's Sweet & Simple Jewelry*. You can follow more of her work at www.aimeeray.com.

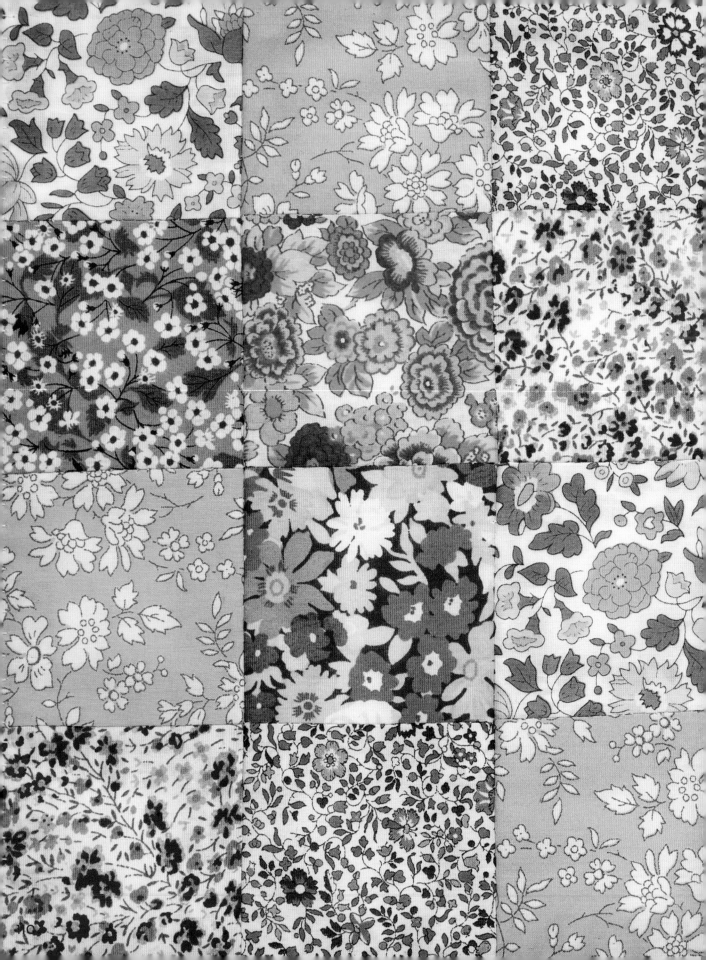

INDEX

HAPPY SEWING!